The Battle for Lives and Souls

The Battle for Lives and Souls

Alan Ames

The decree of the *Congregation of the Propagation of the Faith*, A.A.S 58, 1186 (approved by Pope Paul VI on October 14, 1966) states that the Nihil Obstat and Imprimatur are no longer required on publications that deal with private revelations, provided that they contain nothing contrary to faith and morals.

The publisher recognizes and accepts that the final authority regarding the contents of this book rests with the Holy See of Rome, to whose judgment we willingly submit.

No portion of this book may be copied without the express permission of the author.

Copyright Carver Alan Ames 2011

Layout and design:
Andreas Zureich, Switzerland

ISBN 978-0-9820329-6-1

Dedicated
to all the innocents

Contents

Foreword 11

The Change Began 13

The Sign of Evil 15

Free Love 19

Against the very Nature of Man 25

When I want and what I want 31

Self-centred Society 37

Lack of Respect 41

The Faith under Attack 45

Emptiness of Soul 53

The Pendulum 57

The Green Parties 61

The Solution 67

The Pillars of Faith 73

Interview 77

Messages 87
- Angels 87
- A Pilgrimage 88
- Beautiful Gifts 89
- Children 90
- Confusion 90
- Creation 90
- Darkness 91
- Death 91
- Disagreements 92
- Easter Time 92
- Emptiness 96
- Enjoyment 96
- Error 96
- Equality 96
- Eternal Life 97
- Family 97
- Fear 98
- Following the Lord 99
- Freedom of Choice 100
- Gentle 100
- Gifts 101
- Glory 101
- Good and Evil 102
- Hearts 104
- Heaven 107
- Helping Others 108
- Holiness 108
- Holy Scripture 108
- Humour 109
- Joy 109
- Knowledge 109
- Life 110

Lost Souls	111
Love	112
Making the Effort	113
Marriage	113
Men and Women	116
Mistakes	116
Money	116
Mother Mary	117
Mystery	118
Needs	118
Others	118
Pentecost	120
Pleasing to God	121
Poverty	121
Pride	122
Priests	122
Prisoners	122
Remembering	122
Sacrifice	123
Saints	123
Salvation	124
Service	125
Sin	126
Sorrow	127
Suffering	128
The Church	128
The Cross	131
The End of Time	131
The Eucharist	132
The Faith	132
The Future	133
The Hands of Christ	133
The Love of God	134

The Person	135
The Power of God	136
The Rosary	136
The Sick	137
The Truth	137
The Victory	138
The Way	139
Through the Apostles	139
Truth	140
Trust	141
United	141
Violence	142
Weakness	142
Wisdom	142
Worry	142
Worship	143

Foreword

IN THE ENCLOSED writings are some reflections on what God has shown me and on what I have experienced in my meetings with peoples of different faiths and cultures.

It has become clear to me what is happening in the world, for by God's grace I have been able to look past the superficial and to see what is really happening in the world.

The wonderful thing is that no matter how far away from God we are or no matter how much we reject Him, God is always there waiting to help us put right what is wrong in life and in the world. All it takes is for each person to make the effort in committing themselves to truly living for The Lord, Jesus Christ.

No matter what evil throws at mankind the truth remains clear that the gates of hell cannot stand against The One Holy Catholic and Apostolic Church and that is why it is so important that Catholics live their faith and share it with all they meet. Regardless of how desperate the situation in the world may seem at times we should cling to this truth and help others to do so as well. While society may shift with the sands of public opinion Catholics must stand firm on the rock of faith given in St. Peter and those who have followed in his chair if Catholics truly are to change and help save many in the loving truth of Christ, Our Lord.

The Change Began

During the time of the Vietnam war and the cold war a movement arose within the U.S.A. and spread to other countries. Many people were frustrated with the way their governments were leading them and the lives being wasted and lost in war.

People wanted and expected better from those who led them. Young men and women did not want to put their lives at risk for what they saw as either a war they disagreed with or a war that was more to do with power and politics than freedom. People did not want a growth in nuclear weapons that may lead to nuclear war.

A movement of rebellion grew and the establishment started to be seen as the enemy by some. People called for change and were no longer prepared to accept the way things were. Some of the young believed they were being shackled by the older generation and denied the freedoms they desired. So a movement was born with the aim to change society and hopefully usher in an era of peace and love to replace what many saw as a corrupt system of greed, exploitation and bigotry.

There were good intentioned people on both sides of the argument hoping for a better and freer future of peace, love and harmony. However, each side had differing views on how this would be achieved and frequently both sides viewed the other as the enemy. Emotions often ran high and at times led those who were seeking peace into violent acts. The establishment in uncertainty and fear of the order of society collapsing responded some times in ways which were authoritarian and abuses of power. In the confusion of the age society began to change and change radically. However, the ideal of peace was never achieved, lives are still being lost in wars. True freedom was not found as people, while freed from the perceived chains of the times, have shackled themselves in other ways. The promise of a better future has not been fulfilled for still there is inequality, poverty and oppression.

Interestingly, some of the same people who called for change then are the ones now behaving in the similar ways as those they previously criticized. Some of those who wanted to eradicate corruption have become the corrupted, the greedy, the exploiters and the bigots and are blind to the fact that they are. Some of those who called for a better future have led society into a worse one.

It is true that there was much that needed changing in society but also there was much that did not need to change. Sadly many good ways were discarded in the desire to get rid of the bad.

Both sides are to blame for this as if the establishment had not forced people into fighting in war, had not stifled the freedom seeking hearts of the people, had treated people not as subjects but as partners in society, had not deceived people with the many untruths they told and had seen all as equal then there would have been no great movement of peace and love. It would not have been needed.

The Sign of Evil

IN THIS ATMOSPHERE of confusion and uncertainty it is plain to see the hand of the evil one at work. Evil when possible will use the good intentions of people to lead them into sin. Evil will hide darkness behind what seems good so as to draw people into its grasp. Evil used the desire for peace, love and a fair society as the means to lead people into the dark. Yet, Satan made it very obvious that he was at work for he gave the people a symbol to wear and to march behind, a symbol that was clearly from him but most did not recognize it because they were too blind to see.

The symbol he gave was the inverted cross in a circle which so many came to embrace and still do. This sign stamped the evil one's mark on this movement but so few noticed it.

This symbol is anti – Christ for it has His Holy cross upside down inside the circle, which is a representation of God, for like God a circle has no beginning and no end. This symbol is also a rejection of Catholicism as on some of the priest's robes

 (Chasuble) the cross is this shape but the correct way up. This symbol is a mark of the beast and how interesting it is that many look for the mark of the beast and yet when it is put before them openly and for all to see they do not recognize it. Here clearly the evil one said to the world this is my movement and so few noticed … and still so few notice. Many Christians have and still do embrace this sign of evil and do not understand where it originates from and that it is a direct attack on Christianity. Many cry out from behind this symbol for peace and a better society not realizing that the evil one is working to bring only turmoil and a worse society, not realizing that the evil one has declared war on society.

Evil attacks that which it hates and that is belief in God, morals, families and human life itself. In his cunning the evil one sugar coats the poison pills of sinfulness and leads many into the darkness through sin and the acceptance of it.

Slowly but surely evil has changed mankind's perception of sin so that immorality pervades society and that which would be rejected in the past because it is wrong is now accepted and openly promoted, even in times taught in schools as normal. It seems so few in society recognize sin and the fruits it brings. Many have been deceived into believing the foolish arguments evil has used to gain approval for what is obviously wrong. Many have been led away from the truth of God into believing in the old pagan ways, which are called *New Age* when in fact there is nothing new in them. Many who proclaim they seek peace and love have been led to reject The Lord, Jesus, who is true love and true peace. Many are drawn into self-centred beliefs instead of God centred beliefs.

Then as society disintegrates and bad behaviour becomes the norm some of these same people wonder why. A civilised society must have good morals at its core otherwise society becomes disordered and uncivil and it is plain to see that is what has happened in many societies today. The lack of civility and respect for one another is rampant. So often people just think of themselves and what they see as their rights forgetting the rights of others. The foulest of language is used even by the very young. Disgusting acts, which are at times done openly and publicly, are praised and promoted by some. Ways of life that go against the very nature of man are given protection by law and are forced upon society. What a mess the world is in and so much of it caused by the ones who wanted to make the world a better place but instead have made it far worse.

When people think of themselves first and seek to satisfy their own desires regardless of the consequences then society becomes worse. Hearts become cold to others in need and become empty of true love for where selfishness is there cannot be true love. Every heart longs for love and so when a heart is denied love it hungers for it. This hunger can lead people to feed their hearts with that which may at times cover up the ache of the heart but never truly removes it. The false love found in immorality gives some comfort at times but a comfort that does not last. Addictive substances seem to satisfy for a while but again this does not last. Money and things of the world bring fleeting satisfaction but no true peace and contentment. Today so many hearts are hungry for love because the way of life many lead is the wrong way and is the way that brings only false love and loneliness into hearts.

The promise for a better future evil seemed to offer through this movement of change appeared good but truly never was and so often only bore rotten fruit. Today society pays a high price for the foolishness of those who embraced sinful ways and yet so few are prepared to recognize this and do anything to change it.

Free Love

FREE LOVE WITH a permissive society was one of the calls of the times with phrases such as *Make love not war*, used to promote this ideal. However, free love was and is not free it has made slaves of many. Free love has cost many a high price indeed. Sex is now seen by some as no more than a physical act of self-satisfaction rather than the true expression of love it is meant to be. As people began to explore sexuality in what they saw as a right to do so much was lost. Respect quickly faded as people began to look upon one another as objects to satisfy their sexual desires. Numerous men and women began to experience a variety of sexual partners and in doing so lost the true intimacy of love. In the sampling of the many it became harder for people to be satisfied with one partner as the bond of love was and is not in the relationships they have. Instead the false love that comes with immorality and that usually only lasts for a short time replaces that which is good and holy. It is no wonder that in society today there are so many lonely people for some have made themselves lonely in their embrace of immorality.

It is so hard now for people to find and form true relationships as they do not know what a true relationship is. Some only know going from one partner to another. Some stay with a person until they are bored with them and then leave. Many today do not have good marriages because they are not satisfied within the marriage as they think of self and their desires and put them before all else. Many want to have the excitement of what they think is love, but is no more than passion, with them every day. So when it is not they look elsewhere. Adultery is commonplace as people seek to bring a bit more excitement and pleasure into their lives this of course is just another expression of selfishness. Some marry several times seeing marriage as nothing more than a relationship that can be broken at any time for any reason. There seems to be little desire to work at marriage to make it successful, instead when problems come some people decide to divorce and look for an easier life else where. In a lot of marriages today people are less prepared to sacrifice and without sacrifice marriage cannot work. Some seek perfection in their spouse not understanding they themselves are imperfect, and when they do not find it, divorce and look elsewhere. Some in their vanity and selfishness look for younger partners and leave the one they are with. Some then find that they are left alone as their looks fade with time. To hear people in their later years talking of their new boyfriend or new girlfriend sounds like a sad joke. To see those married several times and now alone in their life is to see a sadness that was avoidable. Now because no true loving relationship in a true marriage was formed many are left alone as they age.

So often it is the children who suffer when a marriage falls apart. They see their parents arguing, showing little love. The children at times feel it is they who are being rejected or that maybe it is their fault that the parents separate. Then there are the many cases of domestic violence caused by the break up of marriages. One or both of the parents or the children may be attacked and injured, killed or may commit suicide. Separated parents frequently say the children will be fine that they will cope. This is not true because all children when the family falls apart are affected badly in some way be it emotional, spiritual or physical. Some of these children as they grow find it hard to have good and loving relationships. Marriage not surprisingly is seen by some of the young as unnecessary because they have been set such bad examples by their elders.

In the call for sexual liberation it was encouraged that people should live together first to see if they are compatible and that this would also help reduce divorce. This of course was another of evil's deceptions which said it is alright to live with someone and have a sexual relationship and if it does not work out just leave. Because there is not the full commitment of love needed in the relationship of course in many cases it will not work out. In living together the people are saying to each other I am not prepared to give you all of myself in true love, I will hold something back. The suggestion of fewer divorces was not fulfilled as divorce rates have skyrocketed. So this deception is an obvious failure but still people in thoughts of self and being unprepared to totally commit them selves to another person embrace it.

Sexual liberation has also led people to accept the unacceptable. As people began to have free sex one of the natural consequences is that there would be more pregnancies. Now of course because people saw it as a right to have sex with who ever they wanted whenever they wanted, a desire for contraception was born in the hearts of many. They did not want children to spoil the enjoyment they were having, what right have children to do that? Some people want to have sex without consequences and without children to burden them. So contraception became widespread and used by many. Even within marriages contraception is used to prevent unwanted children that might be a burden on the family. Children, it is thought, take up time, restrict the parents' social life, cost a lot to feed and clothe. Children are a responsibility many do not want to have while they have time to enjoy them selves in life. Foetuses are screened for genetic diseases and terminations recommended for those children in the womb who may have a flaw in the eyes of man. The thought is that if they are born they will be a heavy cross and an unnecessary one. I recently read that approximately 90% of Downs Syndrome babies are aborted!

Once again selfishness reared its ugly head in the lives of some. Because abortion had become legalized in various places and the numbers of abortions were increasing due to the immoral behaviour of people contraception was also seen as a way to prevent and reduce abortions. This again has proved to be untrue as the number of abortions continues to climb. The number of babies killed rises.

FROM THE JANUARY issue of the international reproductive health journal Contraception:

Trends in the use of contraceptive methods and voluntary interruption of pregnancy in the Spanish population during 1997–2007

This study was designed to acquire information about the use of contraceptive methods in order to reduce the number of elective abortions.

Since 1997, representative samples of Spanish women of childbearing potential (15–49 years) have been surveyed by the Daphne Team every 2 years to gather data of contraceptive methods used.

During the study period, 1997 to 2007, the overall use of contraceptive methods increased from 49.1% to 79.9%. The most commonly used method was the condom (an increase from 21% to 38.8%), followed by the pill (an increase from 14.2% to 20.3%). Female sterilization and IUDs decreased slightly and were used by less than 5% of women in 2007. The elective abortion rate increased from 5.52 to 11.49 per 1000 women.

The factors responsible for the increased rate of elective abortion need further investigation.

What sort of society kills its own children just so that life styles can be better? A selfish one! The foolishness is that now the societies that have embraced this abomination are finding there are not enough young people to support their aging societies. This should be no surprise ... if you kill the young eventually there will be an imbalance in society. With the disregard for the lives of the young innocents has come a disregard for life in general. The older generation is faced with the prospect of euthanasia, as the calls for it grow louder. The old are now seen by some as burdens on society that drain resources. It seems to matter little that many of the old worked most of their lives paying taxes and building society and caring for the adults of today. This is so often forgotten as the old are looked upon as a problem rather than the treasure they are. It is not only the old who are faced with this but those who have serious diseases and cannot care for themselves or do not have the quality of life that society says people should have. Some governments are reluctant to pay for the palliative care needed for those in severe pain and may see euthanasia as an alternative especially if the person has a terminal disease. It seems now in many cases people are only seen as worthwhile if they are healthy and productive.

Free love, has cost and is costing a lot. The number of sexually transmitted diseases has increased substantially. Apart from ruining lives and relationships STDs also cost society a large amount in the drugs used to treat them and the care needed for those who suffer from some of the worst STDs. It seems that monogamy or a reduction of sexual partners is a very effective way of stopping the spread of STDs yet how that is ridiculed at times by some even though the evidence is there. In Zimbabwe recently a study found:

HARARE, Zimbabwe, February 15, 2011 (LifeSiteNews.com) – Despite the proliferation of massive condom campaigns in the fight against HIV/AIDS, another study has shown that the most effective strategy is to promote marital fidelity and sexual responsibility.

The new study from Zimbabwe, where HIV prevalence has dropped 50% since peaking in the late 1990s, found that the success was driven primarily by changes in sexual behaviour, particularly a drop in casual, commercial, and extramarital sex.

"In Zimbabwe, as elsewhere, partner reduction appears to have played a crucial role in reversing the HIV epidemic," wrote Daniel Halperin, PhD, of the Harvard School of Public Health, and colleagues. The study, published this month at PLoSMedicine.org, was commissioned by the UNFPA and UNAIDS.

Against the very Nature of Man

THE SEXUAL REVOLUTION has drawn people into sex without love and because of this sex cannot be experienced as it should for sex is much more than a physical act. Sex without the emotional, loving and spiritual is just an empty act that cannot satisfy completely. That is why so many of those who are seeking only the physical soon become bored or not content in their sexual activity. Some then seek to expand their sex life by trying new ways of sex. Of course every new way no matter how exciting it may seem does not fill the emptiness of heart. In the seeking of satisfaction some embrace that which go against the very nature of man. Homosexuality has become commonplace with same sex relationships openly promoted in society. Even the young are being educated to accept homosexuality as a normal relationship as an acceptable alternative.

In March 2011 there was a report in the UK called "Too Much, Too young." that revealed the explicit nature of sex education material that groups are pushing onto children as young as 5 years old. They include teaching children about oral and anal sex, prostitution, masturbation, heterosexuality and homosexuality. There are depictions of sexual intercourse and footage of full frontal nudity.

While homosexuals should not be discriminated against or persecuted a true follower of Christ can never accept or endorse homosexual acts. It is also to be remembered that there are various causes for this disorder and not always is it just lustful desires that lead to homosexuality. With the use of oral contraceptives some studies suggest that the hormones within oral contraceptives through excretion enter the water system that all use and so become ingested by many. These hormones and other chemicals found in some plastics and other products when absorbed can have a gender bending effect on those who unknowingly ingest them and so create a change in the hormonal balance leading to a feminization of some men and making some women more masculine.

According to a UCSF study released January 14th 2011: The study, published in the journal *Environmental Health Perspectives,* marks the first time that the number of chemicals to which pregnant women are exposed has been counted, the authors said.

Of the 163 chemicals studied, 43 of them were found in virtually all 268 pregnant women in the study. They included polychlorinated biphenyls or PCBs, a prohibited chemical linked to cancer and other health problems; organochlorine pesticides; polybrominated diphenyl ethers, banned compounds used as flame retardants; and phthalates, which are shown to cause hormone disruption.

Some of these chemicals were banned before many of the women were even born.

It is important to treat homosexuals with compassion and understanding but never accepting their way of life as a right way and always trying to lead those with this disorder to a good way of life. Sadly society in many instances tries to force people to accept what is obviously wrong. In some countries it is called homophobic and discriminatory just to speak the truth about this disorder. In various countries people who have bed and breakfast or similar businesses cannot refuse by law for homosexuals to stay in their rooms even if the owner of the house is totally opposed to homosexuality due to religious or moral beliefs.

January 2011 ... a gay couple in England wins a court case against hoteliers as court awards compensation of £1,800 each to gay couple refused a double room at Chymorvah private hotel in Cornwall.

Devout Christian hotel owners who refused to allow a gay couple to share a double room acted unlawfully, a judge at Bristol county court ruled.

It seems however that even homosexuals are discriminatory and that may be acceptable. Here is a crazy example:

June 2011, Associated Press SEATTLE (AP) – A federal judge in Seattle says a gay softball organization can limit the number of heterosexual players on each team.
The North American Gay Amateur Athletic Alliance oversees gay softball leagues in dozens of U.S. cities and runs an annual tournament called the Gay Softball World Series. Three men claim in a lawsuit that their team's second-place finish in the 2008 tournament in Washington state was nullified because they are bisexual, not gay, and thus their team exceeded the limit of two non-gay players.
U.S. District Judge John Coughenour ruled this week that the organization has a First Amendment right to limit the number of

heterosexual players. However, the judge did say that questions remain about the way the softball association applied its rule, and so the case can proceed

In the U.S.A the month of June has been officially declared by the president to be lesbian, gay, bi-sexual and transsexual pride month ... who in their right mind takes pride in sin but then of course pride itself is part of the problem of mankind.

Because of the acceptance of homosexuality many of the young are confused, they see famous people, rock stars, movie stars and those they idolize sometimes performing homosexual acts as part of their shows or movies or openly promoting homosexuality. To some it has become fashionable to be homosexual. Now same sex couples see it as their right to adopt children or to have them by in vitro fertilization at times even using surrogate mothers to do so. The media report on some of these events as if they are wonderful instead of reporting them for the immoral things they are. Of course regardless of the situation children born by in vitro fertilization or through surrogates with egg implants are loved and treasured by God. It is not the child's fault that they were conceived in immoral ways. The child is guilty of nothing but the parents and those who perform these terrible procedures certainly are. Yet society even at times celebrate when same sex couples adopt or have children born in these ways. How blind have we become? A child needs both a father and a mother not two fathers or two mothers. It is the natural order of creation that a child has a mother and a father. God in His wonderful love and wisdom made it this way. Mankind however in its selfishness rejects what God gives to mankind in the true order and brings disorder into being. It is a real sorrow that children will be brought up and guided in their years of formation by those living in serious error. How will these children ever learn true morals? How will these children be given the opportunity to grow up to be the well balanced people they are meant to be? Sadly in some so-called Christian countries adoption agencies are forced by the government to adopt children out to same sex couples. It is considered discriminatory not to do so. Even the Catholic Church agencies are not exempt to this and some have had to close rather than be forced into what is a serious wrong.

Rome, Italy, April 28, 2011 / 12:58 am (CNA). A Catholic adoption charity in England is facing closure after losing its appeal against a law forcing them to place children with homosexual couples.
Catholic Care, run by the Diocese of Leeds, argued it would have to give up its adoption service if it was not made exempt from the law. However their case has now been rejected by England's Charity Tribunal.

The madness of evil in this is also seen by a judgement in England where a Christian couple were refused fostering a child because they did not approve of homosexuality. A ruling by two judges of the Nottingham Crown Court that described the couple's traditional Christian view of sexuality as "inimical to the interests of children," indicating it could endanger a child's welfare.

A few years ago I was in the U.S.A. and I met a young man in his teenage years. His maternal grandmother had brought him to my talk and for healing prayers. This young man had attempted suicide and almost succeeded but his grandmother had saved him. The cause for his unhappiness was that his mother, in a same sex relationship, decided with her partner that they should have a child. To achieve this they had three of their homosexual male friends donate sperm and the woman was artificially inseminated with all three so that she would not know who the father was. When the boy, who was the result of this procedure, became a teenager he wanted to know who his father was and when his mother told him what she had done he spiralled into depression. He became suicidal at the thought of how he was conceived and did not want to live anymore. Thankfully his grandmother discovered him as he was dying and got him to hospital where he was revived.

This boy told me he felt worthless and something just created to satisfy his mother's desires, he just knew inside of himself what his mother had done was wrong and he was disgusted by it. He felt totally lost and was full of turmoil and bad feelings. With the help of his grandmother and by the grace of God the young man has now overcome these feelings and has begun to live a good life knowing God loves him.

When I want and what I want

A WEB OF evil has and continues to spread across the world from the foolishness of the people wanting to spread peace and love but doing so in the wrong ways. If you step back and look at some of the fruits of those times it would be hard to believe mankind could be so stupid. For instance so many women had abortions as they did not want those children at that particular time. So many people using contraception to prevent pregnancy as they did not want children at that time. So many putting off having children until they are much older as they preferred to have careers or wanted to be free to enjoy themselves. In their enjoyment the spreading and increase of sexually transmitted diseases and with the increase in STDs infertility has increased. Some of these same people when they decide it is right for them, it fits into their schedule, try for children and find it hard to conceive. What did they expect? I meet so many people who have trouble conceiving and a lot, not all, fit into these categories. Of course there are other reasons as well such as bad lifestyles or medical conditions preventing conception. Allan Pacey a senior lecturer of andrology at the university of Sheffield, said; "The social changes over the last 30 to 40 years dwarf any genetic effect. The obesity problem, chlamydia and the tendencies for smaller families and older mothers are having more of an effect on fertility than any genetics."

Sometimes people turn to the immorality of IVF to conceive, they are so desperate now and crave to have what they did not want before. In Vitro Fertilization or IVF is part of the decay of society and its morals. However, a lot of people, Christians included, do not see it that way. Catholics should read the catechism of the Catholic Church and see that IVF is gravely immoral and morally unacceptable. The way IVF has been presented is the way evil often presents wrongs, as if it is something good, something that is a right. Some believe that IVF is good because it helps childless couples have children. While it is a great sadness when married couples cannot have children this does not justify IVF. Infertility is a great cross for many but to try and lift that cross using sinful ways only puts the cross onto others. Such as the embryos discarded when the fertilized eggs are no longer required. The babies used for stem cell research. The embryos experimented on. The embryos frozen and stored until they are required to be implanted into a woman. The babies conceived so they can be donors for a sibling with a disease. The babies discarded because they are not the right sex. The local news is reporting on a story in the state of Victoria in Australia where a couple are seeking a tribunal ruling that they can choose the sex of their baby to be conceived by IVF. The couple want a girl as they already have 3 boys. The woman became pregnant with a girl who died shortly after birth. So the woman again became pregnant with twins through IVF but both were boys so she had the twin babies aborted because they were not girls. Now she wants to be impregnated again through IVF but only with a girl. It seems some people forget that children are gifts from God and that the child is not owned by the parents but given into their safe-keeping. The child is not an object there to satisfy an adult's longing or to be used and abused as the people or the world so desire.

In another shocking case a famous Australian actress who is a Catholic and her husband had a fertilized egg (a baby) implanted into a surrogate *gestational* carrier. "No words can adequately convey the incredible gratitude that we feel for everyone who was so supportive throughout this process, in particular our gestational carrier," they said.

Infertility is a substantial problem in the world but the way some try to fix that problem only makes greater problems. Instead of first looking to what is causing infertility in some people and trying to change that it seems it is preferred to treat the bad result of the causes. A whole industry has grown through IVF, an industry which tries to portray itself as doing good, as helping those in need but in truth it is an industry which is built upon and maintains that which is seriously wrong. Babies now are becoming commodities that are exploited and used to exploit. It is an industry that is also self perpetuating as there is a high rate of infertility among those born by IVF because they may inherit their parents fertility problems so these if they want children themselves may need IVF.

Many people do not accept the truth of life that when an egg is fertilized it is a child; that it is a person. The child is seen by some as nothing more than cells to be manipulated in any way mankind sees fit. The child's rights are ignored and the wrongs of the world supersede the child's rights. Here again is evil at work devaluing life and getting mankind to abuse and even destroy its own children. Sadly there is a group of people that cannot have children but some are not prepared to accept that. Some believe they can have what they want, when they want, how they want, regardless of what they have to do to get it. Infertility in itself is not evil but the ways of treating it such as IVF certainly are. The love of husband and wife in marriage in the act of procreation is the way God wants babies to be conceived. It is in this union of love that God's will for bringing human life into the world is fulfilled. The treatment of human infertility is to be encouraged and applauded but only when it does not involve methods or techniques which are against the design and will of God.

Others look to adopt but there are few babies to adopt in their own countries because of the very same reasons they embraced before so some look overseas for children but often do not get them. Unfortunately this is a suffering some have brought upon themselves. People end up with no children and become depressed, unhappy with life and feel empty within because they cannot have a family. They cannot have what they did not want before and they are not prepared to accept that or know how to cope with that. Some even try to buy babies from the poorer countries and do not see how sinful and selfish this behaviour is in itself. There are reports of babies being stolen from families to be sold to childless couples and poor families being forced by their poverty to sell their own children in desperation. Once again here is the hand of evil spreading pain and suffering. Some of those who do this think it is the best for the child but it never is in a child's best interest to take it from its family unless of course the child is being abused. It is always best for a child to grow up in its own loving family.

Anyone with a true heart and mind can see the way evil is working through abortion and contraception to destroy society. Families damaged and broken. The spread of disease and unhappiness. Loneliness in old age where there are no children or grandchildren. Too few young to keep up the productivity needed for economies to function correctly. Too few young to fill the gaps left by those retiring or dying. Too few young to care for and to finance the care of the elderly. The twin evils of abortion and contraception are tools the evil one uses in an attempt to get mankind to destroy itself. The evil one revels in the suffering of mankind. He treasures the hurt and pain the foolish bring upon themselves in the embrace of sinful selfish ways and the sacrificing of their children and their future. Yet, still many are blind to this and continue to accept and promote these evils.

Self-centred Society

EVIL HAS BROUGHT the focus of many people onto self so as to take the focus from God.

Simple things that may sound to some as if they are right but in truth are very wrong have been used to create a self-centred society. *Do what you like as long as it hurts no one,* to some sounds reasonable because they do not understand in doing what you want often means embracing sin in various forms. It suggests do what you want and anything is justified as long as others are not injured. Yet when people do what they want sexually people are hurt emotionally, sometimes physically and spiritually. How many wives or husbands are hurt by adultery? How many people are hurt when they are taken advantage of sexually and then discarded, when the person they may love but does not love them, no longer has a desire for them?

Do what you want also has led many people to experiment with illegal drugs. Some say they take drugs and it only affects them, it has nothing to do with anyone else. They say that drugs bring them wonderful experiences that are pleasurable. They should be free to use drugs as they like. Who has the right to say they should not? Of course this is all about self and the truth is that when people are drawn into the darkness of drugs of addiction many are hurt, many are affected. The rights of others are never truly considered by those who take drugs of addiction. The drug addicts often lose any respect they have for others. The rights of the families that they come from which so often are broken because of the drug users actions. The parents whose children become different people and treat their mothers and fathers terribly, often stealing from the family and friends to get the money to feed their need for drugs. The pain of parents whose children die from or are killed because of illegal drugs. The cost to society with the violence and crime associated with drugs and drug use. The cost of medical treatment for drug addicts.

Then there is the effect on the person themselves with health problems. The loss of self respect as so many think little of themselves after a while and at times are prepared to do anything to get the drugs they desire. So many become prostitutes, thieves, liars, manipulators or beggars on the street with no home to go to. So many commit suicide or die of accidental overdoses or from the diseases associated with drug taking. I wonder at times how people can be so blind and so foolish. A person only has to look and see does anyone who is addicted to drugs really benefit from it. All have problems rich and poor alike. Drugs do not improve life except for some of those evil people making money from selling and distributing them. Drugs of addiction make life worse for those who use them yet still so many experiment with drugs. Who can you look at and say it was drugs that made them successful, healthy and a good person? Who can you look at and say thank God they took heroin or cocaine it really helped them be a better person, it helped them have better morals and to behave better? While you can see many using drugs and glorifying drug use you cannot truly see any benefit from drugs of addiction. But then isn't this the way of evil; use something that at first may bring some pleasure but in the end always has a high price attached to it and for some that price is their very soul. Most of the drug addicts and the drug users truly are selfish people who put their own pleasure, their desires before anything or anyone else. Many know what they do is wrong but they try to hide or deny this truth using all sorts of foolish justifications for their weakness. To help ease their consciences or to make what they do more acceptable or even legal not only drug users but also homosexuals, abortionists and many others doing wrong try to persuade or even force society to approve of their actions. For once accepted by society then those doing wrong feel vindicated. That they were right and their bad actions are not bad at all, it is just that some bigots or religious fanatics opposed their way of life. Those who live in a bad way also try to draw other people into their way of life for they seem to think the more people doing what they do the more justified it is. Also beneath this is the action of evil working through the weaknesses of those living in a bad way to lead others into a bad life. Evil wants as many people to suffer as possible so the evil one gives the warped desire to some to draw others into their suffering; some believing their suffering shared is their suffering lessened. It is like a cancer spreading through society.

Lack of Respect

THE LACK OF respect is not only among those who have addictions to substances but is becoming ingrained in society. People do not respect themselves and that is plain to see by the behaviour in the world today. The lack of self-respect can be seen in the relationships many have with others as the person lets their body be used as if it is of little value when in fact our bodies are wonderful gifts of love given by God and to be treasured. Yet, so many do not respect their own bodies in the immoral ways they use them. Bodies filled with substances of addiction. Bodies disfigured with all sorts of piercings in the eyelids, ears, nose, mouth, lips, tongue, breasts, stomach and genital areas. Bodies covered in tattoos. (The plastic surgeons must be looking ahead in great anticipation to the time when many of those with tattoos will want them removed!) Bodies disrespected by the way people dress, which can make some look as if they work in brothels and yet it is called fashion!

It is interesting that a great number seem to be addicted to shopping and saying things like *shop till you drop*. For some shopping has become one of the main focuses in their lives. They have to have the latest and best whatever it is. Be it computers, phones, sneakers, and clothes etc. Yet with so many buying the latest fashions as I walk the streets in some countries people seem to dress in unkempt and scruffy ways. It is hard at times to see a well-dressed person. Where are all the clothes people have bought? Why are people going and buying so many clothes and still look scruffy? This addiction to shopping is just another sign of the emptiness within that many have because they live in ways that cannot possibly fill the soul. So they try to fill the emptiness with things that cannot fill, but just soothes for a while. Sadly in this addiction the person who has it often wastes as they buy that which they do not truly need. In doing so they are not only wasting their own resources but also wasting that which could be used to help those in need. If, instead of buying something that is used once or twice and then put aside or buying something that was unnecessary the money was used to help the poor, then the money would be used in a good way instead of a selfish wasteful way. There is nothing wrong with shopping except if the shopping is done to excess and is wasteful. We all need clothes etc., but how many do we need? How many shirts do we need to wear? How many dresses do we truly need? How many pairs of shoes? Sadly many do not ask themselves this question and answer it truthfully. Many do not have the self-restraint needed to control themselves because society promotes a lack of self-restraint and encourages people to get whatever they want. Self first and whatever you want is what society in various countries teaches today. There has also been a lack of discipline in the lives of the young as some of the so called *free thinkers* believe children should be allowed to express themselves without any barriers. When children are not given some guidelines and taught what is appropriate and what is not then they cannot learn how to behave properly. No wonder the young are so confused. No wonder so many of the young get lost in life for they have few good examples to follow. In the movies, on television, in the music and the games they play there are many bad examples and bad role models. If the young are not given a clear understanding of what is right and what is wrong how can we expect them to behave in good ways? If those the young have had placed before them as role models promote bad behaviour by their own bad behaviour can we expect any different from the young? How can parents expect their children to respect them if the parents in their own lives are not respectful of others, of life and of self?

Bad language is commonplace and words that would have been condemned in the past for the disgrace they are have become part of everyday vocabulary. Insulting language full of expletives is the language many in society use and see no wrong in it. There has been a dumbing down of society and this is reflected in the way people speak to each other. Why people believe it is funny or acceptable to be abusive in words is hard to understand except when you look and see the hand of evil at work. Evil does not want people to speak nicely, it prefers bad language. Bad words are one of the evil one's instruments used to lower moral standards and reduce respect for one another. Evil also can use bad words to hurt, to insult, to upset, to offend or to cause problems and foolishly many people become his vessels for doing so. Instead of being polite and gracious, people in their words have become abusive and vile. Bad words only reflect the darkness and confusion within and lowers the person speaking them not only morally but spiritually too. If a person cannot say a good word they should say nothing. Bad words show the immaturity, the foolishness and the moral decay of people. Foul words open hearts and souls to evil just as good and holy words open hearts and souls to God.

In the past many of the young looked to the saints for their inspiration in life today however, it seems the saints have been replaced in many lives as role models by the rich, the famous, the prideful and the self-centred. The entertainers, the famous and the wealthy often believe they are something special, better than others, because society has placed them on pedestals and encouraged them to have these false beliefs about themselves. It seems the good role models are few and far between and those who do act in good ways or promote good and wholesome lifestyles are often attacked for doing so. Some are called religious fanatics, extremists, old-fashioned, out of touch or just plain crazy. They are mocked, abused and even attacked physically at times for promoting what is good. But then isn't that what evil has always done to good people.

Those who called for tolerance in the past have in many cases become the new intolerant. If people do not accept the new ideologies and the new lifestyles promoted by the immoral then the moral are seen as bigots, as denying people their rights. Yet, the rights of the moral people are given little consideration if any at all. The moral are now the ones who are being discriminated against in some countries as the immoral influence governments have and what is wrong sometimes becoming government policy. To oppose these policies can mean fines, losing of a job or even imprisonment. Yet, the very same people who in the past were calling for an end to oppression now oppress those who do not agree with them and either do not realize what they are doing or just do not care as long as they get their own way.

The Faith under Attack

THE EQUALITY MANY sought in the past has become an equality that only sees those who agree with the immoral as equal and the others as not worth listening to; sees the others as intellectually inferior. An equality that says in some countries you can no longer wear the symbols of your faith around your neck as it may offend those who do not believe and it does not matter about your rights or your freedom of faith or expression. An equality that allows those with immoral agendas to have freedom of speech and expression regardless of how it offends those of faith. Yet, if those of faith speak out against what is wrong they can be prosecuted for being homophobic even for being pro-life.

March 22nd 2011, GENEVA (Reuters) – People who criticise gay sexual relations for religious or moral reasons are increasingly being attacked and vilified for their views, a Vatican diplomat told the United Nations Human Rights Council on Tuesday. Archbishop Silvano Tomasi said the Roman Catholic Church deeply believed that human sexuality was a gift reserved for married heterosexual couples. But those who express these views are faced with "a disturbing trend," he said.

"People are being attacked for taking positions that do not support sexual behaviour between people of the same sex," he told the current session of the Human Rights Council.

"When they express their moral beliefs or beliefs about human nature … they are stigmatised, and worse – they are vilified, and prosecuted.

"These attacks are violations of fundamental human rights and cannot be justified under any circumstances," Tomasi said.

It seems freedom of speech is selective and that those who try to live the right ways often have their speech and actions restricted. The truth is that the equality so many sought was never found and one form of inequality was only replaced with another. Now the rights of the moral are denied while the wrongs of the immoral, in many instances, are protected by law and promoted by governments.

It is sad that the immoral can in the name of free speech, art or literacy do that which is highly offensive to Christians as they depict in art form or in words Christ in blasphemous ways and nothing happens to them. It seems people can say and do anything to Christ and His image without any restrictions. What would happen to a Christian if he depicted homosexuals or abortionists in ways that offended them? This of course is illegal in some countries and so the law would step in. However, a true Christian would never do this, as a Christian would use love not insults and offense to change peoples' hearts. It is also very interesting that most of those "so called" brave artists and authors who say they are pushing the boundaries or are defending freedom of expression and speech do not depict Mohammed in the bad ways that Christ is often depicted. They know they can attack Christians and little happens so Christians are easy targets but these people fear Islam and what it would do to them if they mocked or insulted Mohammed. In truth they are no more than bullies and cowards picking on those they see as weak and vulnerable but fearing those who they know will respond in violent ways.

Madrid, Spain, March 11, 2011 / 08:01 pm (CNA). Some 70 college students stormed into the chapel of Madrid's Complutense University on March 10, shouting insults against the Catholic Church, Pope Benedict XVI and priests.
Several females from the group stood on the altar, undressed from the waist up.
Another female student who was in the chapel praying at the time told the Spanish daily ABC that two of the young women on the altar "boasted about their homosexual tendencies."
The group of students stormed into the chapel with a megaphone and pushed the chaplain out of the way. They proceeded to shout insults against the Catholic Church and her teachings. The group also placed posters in the pews and on the bulletin board at the entrance to the chapel. The entire incident was caught on film.
Another student interviewed by ABC asked, "What would have happened had this taken place in a mosque? These people should know that Catholics will never respond to a provocation with another provocation just to defend themselves."
"Nobody will silence us by acting with hostility, mockery, intimidation or any other illegitimate pressure that offends the religions sensibilities of everyone," she continued. "Moreover, acts like these are punishable by law. How easy and cowardly it is to do something like this anonymously!"

It should be of no surprise that one of the main attacks by evil through this movement of change was and continues to be aimed at the Catholic Church, as the evil one hates Catholicism because the One Holy, Catholic and Apostolic Church is the body of Christ. The Church stands firm in the face of evil and does not change with the times but holds onto the unchangeable truth that Christ gave to mankind. No wonder then that the Church comes under such great attacks from evil. Evil tries to portray the Church as out of touch with reality or as full of men who desire to control peoples' lives and abusers of children and who see women as inferior. Yet, the truth is so different as the Church sees all as equal but with different roles to play in fulfilling God's will. The Church holds firm to the reality of spiritual as well as physical truth. The Church speaks out against what is wrong in society and does not sway with the times or public opinion. Unlike other denominations which call themselves Christian, followers of Christ but who refuse to follow Christ's will and instead follow the will of the world. The denominations which accept contraception, abortion, homosexuality, same sex unions, even having openly homosexual ministers and bishops, women ministers and bishops, see little wrong in divorce. They refuse to follow Christs' Word by rejecting that with which they do not agree or even changing His Holy Word to suit them selves.

It was reported in the Daily Mail January 18th 2011 that the Church of England baptism services may be rewritten to remove some references to Christianity.

The plan for a new *baptism lite* service designed to make christenings more interesting to non-churchgoers will be considered next month by the Church's parliament, the General Synod.

In Canada The National Post reported on March 7th 2011: Canadian Anglicans will hold discussions this spring about whether baptism is necessary for taking part in communion – questioning a requirement of Christianity that has existed for 2,000 years.

"Official teaching is you have to be baptized first. But a number of clergy across the country feel strongly about this as an issue and many have approached their bishops about allowing for an 'open table' in which all could take communion," said Archdeacon Paul Feheley, who is the principal secretary to Archbishop Fred Hiltz, head of the Anglican Church of Canada.

These denominations are worldly and secular and have little to do with the true spiritual and physical life that Christ calls all to live. Some of these denominations see themselves as democracies, yet Christ, Our Lord, never took a vote amongst the apostles to decide what to do or what was right or wrong. He lived to the truth of God and showed all how to do the same. He then gave mankind the grace to live to His way if they so desired but sadly so many do not desire and so many do not seek the grace Jesus, Our Lord, offers.

These other denominations have allowed the evil that has swamped the world to wash over their faith and to wash away the will of Christ to be replaced with the will of man. Any faith that puts what mankind wants before that which Christ desires is truly not Christian and is leading others into the same grievous errors that they live to.

It seems even those within other denominations are recognizing their problems and some are becoming Catholic. A report in the National Catholic Register 18th March 2011 states:

Over the past several years, an increasing number of Lutheran theologians have joined the Church's ranks, some of whom now teach at Catholic colleges and universities. They include, but are not limited to: Paul Quist (2005), Richard Ballard (2006), Paul Abbe (2006), Thomas McMichael, Mickey Mattox, David Fagerberg, Bruce Marshall, Reinhard Hutter, Philip Max Johnson, and most recently, Dr. Michael Root (2010) ...

"What some Lutherans were realizing was that, without the moorings of the Church's Magisterium, Lutheranism would ineluctably drift from it's confessional and biblical source," wrote Quist ...

Many of the converts have come from The Society of the Holy Trinity, a pan-Lutheran ministerium organized in 1997 to work for the confessional and spiritual renewal of Lutheran churches.

Now, it appears that a larger Lutheran body will be joining the Church. Father Christopher Phillips, writing at the Anglo-Catholic blog, reports that the Anglo-Lutheran Catholic Church (ALCC) clergy and parishes will be entering into the U.S. ordinariate being created for those Anglicans desiring to enter the Church.

According to the blog, the ALCC sent a letter to Walter Cardinal Kasper, on May 13, 2009, stating that it "desires to undo the mistakes of Father Martin Luther, and return to the One, Holy, and True Catholic Church established by our Lord Jesus Christ through the Blessed Saint Peter." That letter was sent to the Congregation for the Doctrine of the Faith.

That is not to say that there are not problems within the Catholic Church for surely there are. The Catholic Church is full of sinful people and it is to be expected that some will slip into the grasp of evil and that some will do that which will hurt others. The problems within the One Holy, Catholic and Apostolic Church come from people within it not living to the faith as they should but the faith itself is perfect for it is the faith Christ gave to mankind. Unlike in other denominations where it is the faith they have that has errors and flaws within it and it is that faith which leads people into error and away from truth. Of course the world magnifies the problems within the Catholic Church in an attempt to destroy it as some of those in the world abhor the truth of God and will do anything to stop the truth being proclaimed. The recent terrible child abuse scandals are an example. Sadly, priests within the church did commit some disgraceful and shocking acts upon others and need to be held to account for that. However, the number of priests who did this is in comparison to the general public and other religious organisations is relatively small. Yet the media in general and many who are against the church tried to portray it as if abuse was commonplace. Some seemed to think that this was a way of destroying the Catholic Church and that numbers going to church would shrink dramatically. To the surprise of some this has not happened, the numbers are not declining. This is because those within the church while acknowledging the wrongs done see it for what it is; a failing of the person not of the priesthood. It is understood that the priesthood is a sacred gift given by Christ and that His holiness resides within that sacred calling. That does not change because some weak and extremely sinful men become priests. The priesthood is above the weaknesses of man. It is an office bestowed from on high and which, despite the terrible behaviour of some, will continue to be bestowed from on high and will continue to be the office through which Christ, Our Lord, gives mankind the greatest of gifts and blessings.

Emptiness of Soul

WHAT HAS HAPPENED as Christianity has been attacked, devalued and declared irrelevant is that an emptiness of heart and soul has come into the lives of those who turn from, deny, or reject Christ, Our Lord. If a soul is not fed the truth of Christ then it can never be satisfied, it is always restless, it is always hungry and seeks to satisfy this hunger in that which cannot fill. There is a spiritual famine in the world because hearts are closed to the Holy Spirit of God. That is why so many have been drawn into the spirit of New Age, into Eastern belief's, into witchcraft and even into satanism. The soul longs to be satisfied and so the person if not in a relationship with the true God, The Holy Trinity, looks elsewhere. So many today are drawn into beliefs that are self-centred where the person may be encouraged to try and reach higher levels of existence. Where the person may be told that they can eventually reach equality with whatever is presented to them as the divine. There is little talk of sacrificing for others, of helping others reach holy and happy lives; often it is about self and improvement or elevation of self. Some of the beliefs also denigrate mankind and devalue the gift of humanity. Which of course is what evil wants to do. Evil sees mankind as of little value and tries to make people believe the same. This happens by raising animals to the same level as man or even higher as some faiths believe animals are gods i.e. the monkey god, the elephant god. This devaluation of man is also done in the atheistic evolutionary world where it is often suggested that humans are no more than animals and that humans have just developed with a higher level of intelligence than the other animals. Any suggestion that God created man in His image and as superior to animals is scoffed at. This is what the evil one believes and wants mankind to believe and so uses these so-called religions or atheism to bring mankind to accept this.

The new age philosophies are nothing more than a remaking and presenting in different ways the old pagan beliefs. Such as the belief in Mother Earth or a mother god, lunar influences, crystals, the spirits of the animals and plants, control the spirit within so as to use its power, tapping in to the spirit of the universe, the power of various godlike figures and calling on them for power, healing and authority, channelling the spirits etc. All these and various other new age or occult ways have the same old deceptions of the evil one at their core and all lead away from God and lead into the dark.

There is also witchcraft, which in some places is now recognized as a religion. Some people separate wicca from witchcraft but both are from pagan ways and both deny the one true God. Wicca is neo paganism based on a mix of Saxon and/or Celtic folk traditions and ceremonial magic and of course magic is not from God but from evil. The evil one offers people power through the ways of witchcraft and some people in their blindness seek this power, at times believing it makes them someone special, someone above others, someone who can control others and use others. Some in their misunderstanding think they may be able to do good through what is called white witchcraft but no good comes from evil. Even if you alter the name to make evil sound more attractive evil is still evil. Today there are even books and movies based on witchcraft trying to make it seem as if there is no wrong in some forms of witchcraft. Suggesting that witchcraft is exciting and fun. All witchcraft is wrong. All witchcraft comes from evil and from that which denies God. Any power given through witchcraft comes from the power of evil. Any spirits contacted through witchcraft are evil spirits. Any excitement or perceived fun has a price to be paid and for some that price may be their very soul. In the extreme forms of witchcraft there are even animal and human sacrifices; here again is the evil one reaching out to hurt and destroy man. There are also people who embrace satanism in their desire to satisfy the hunger and emptiness they feel within and their desire for power and excitement. They worship the evil one and cannot see how stupid this is. The evil one from the beginning has done all he can to destroy mankind and will not keep any perceived agreement he has made with people. It seems these people who embrace satanism actually believe they will get some kind of reward from the evil one forgetting or not believing all he will give as a reward is eternal suffering.

So, as Christ, Our Lord has been denied, evil has used various ways to replace Him in peoples' lives, ways which lead further into the darkness of evil and the pain that awaits there. How sad it is that some reject God who offers love, peace and happiness and invite into their lives that which only brings misery, suffering and turmoil.

The Pendulum

THERE IS A great risk in the embracing of the immoral cultural changes that have been introduced to mankind through those who sought a better world but sought it in the wrong way. The risk is that there will be a counter movement that will take society further in the opposite direction. It is certain that there are those who do not like the extreme liberalism that many try to impose on society and desire for it to be halted.

The pendulum has swung so far into immorality that it is almost certain there will be a correction. The problem is that instead of having a correction that brings society to its senses and to living as mankind is meant to there could be a correction that brings evil in other forms into society through extreme conservative and nationalistic views.

There are those who because they can find no meaning in life now, as they are not taught or shown true values, look for something to bring sense and order into life and so are open to manipulation by extreme ideologies. There are those who because they do not know the truth of God's love as revealed in Jesus Christ, have turmoil and no peace within and so may accept some other belief in God as truth, a belief which may be extreme and authoritarian.

There is already an authoritarian political system, which under the name of religion seeks to completely control peoples' lives using the name of God to do so. A faith which denies the divinity of Jesus. A faith which forces its will upon people through threats and fear. A faith which says convert or die. A faith which says if a person changes beliefs they are to be killed. A faith that states if a person blasphemes they are to be killed. A faith that does not see all as equal but sees females as less than men. A faith that believes in polygamy. A faith that marries young women to old men and if the girl refuses she can be killed. A religion that allows honour killings for those women who dare to fall in love with a non-believer and want to marry him. A religious system which in various countries that does not want women to be educated. A faith that accepts slavery. A faith that believes in magical spirits such as Gin's or Genies. A faith that states it is acceptable to lie to your enemies and to kill those who do not believe. A faith that stones people to death (the devil is in the detail as it is prescribed that only certain sized stones may be used). A faith where the founder said never make friends with a Christian or a Jew.

Some are foolishly turning to this belief system in their unhappiness with the way society is. It is interesting that numbers of African Americans join this faith as they are angry or upset with the way they have been and are treated in the U.S.A. Some, justifiably at times, complain about the slavery of the past and bad treatment that may be still happening but are blind to the fact that in the world today under the faith they have joined slavery is alive and active, that many people are treated the same if not far worse than the African Americans were and are. Is slavery only wrong when it happens to your own people but acceptable when it is others being enslaved? How many do we hear speaking out against this evil wherever it is and whoever is doing it?

Some see Christianity is to blame for the bad that has happened to them but while Christians may have behaved in terrible ways and treated others badly, the faith Jesus Christ gave to mankind is one that sees all as equal and demands respect for all. It is the faith of peace, love and forgiveness. It is the faith that offers freedom of choice to all as this Holy Catholic faith understands that God has given each person free will and that free will is to be respected even when the people may make the wrong choices.

It is also interesting as I meet many Africans around the world that some claim that this authoritarian belief system is part of their African heritage. How can that be for Christianity was in Africa long before this religion ever existed? As this faith is spreading throughout the world through migration and conversion of those disillusioned with the liberal societies it is possible that in the future those who reject Christ and His gentle and tender love will find themselves forced to do what they do not want to. They will find themselves living under strict laws with little compassion or mercy. The immorality many accept today will be crushed with an iron fist. Women's equality will disappear. There will be no respect for an individual's free will.

Jesus, Christ, in His One Holy, Catholic and Apostolic Church offers mankind true freedom in Him. Yet many reject this offer and are at risk of becoming unwilling subjects of an authoritarian system that allows little freedom and forces all to live in ways that truly are ways of enslavement.

The Green Parties

THERE IS ALSO another movement that is almost like a religion for some and that is the environmental movement. While of course it is important to look after the animals and the environment this has to be kept in perspective. Some see the trees and the animals as of almost equal value as humans, which is not true. Mankind was created by God and placed above the animals and the environment. However, as the Catholic Church teaches, mankind are stewards meant to care for and protect the planet and all of God's creations on it. All of God's creatures are meant to be treated with respect and not exploited and not to be treated badly. Some unfortunately do not do this and abuse what God has given to mankind in His love. If people do not respect one another it is easy not to respect the planet. All should value the world around us but those who place animals and trees etc., on the same level or as important as people in doing so devalue man. Those who see protecting the environment as more important than protecting human life again devalue the great gift of human life given by God. Sadly, in some countries the green movement has become an umbrella under which many causes shelter and promote their agendas. In some countries the green parties support abortion, birth control, homosexuality, gay marriage, euthanasia. The false argument that there are too many people on the planet and that the planet cannot support such a large number of people is in some of the environmentalists' eyes a reason to support abortion and birth control. In Australia the green party, which supports the minority government, insisted in the first weeks of government that gay marriage and euthanasia should be on the agenda before parliament. Obviously very important environmental matters!

It is interesting that some in the green movements use oral contraceptives and seem to give little regard to the chemicals they excrete because of this into the water system. Chemicals such as oestrogen that some studies suggest have a gender bending effect on animals as well as people. So much for the environment!

I am amazed also at those women who spend so much time exercising and are careful as to what they eat and drink such as organic foods so as to stay healthy and avoid chemicals in fruit, meats and vegetables. Some try to eat only organic yet so easily swallow an oral contraceptive. Many turn their backs on or reject natural family planning methods, which of course are healthier and cleaner than taking drugs. Also, natural family methods such as the Billing's method have been shown to be at least as equally effective if not more so than oral contraceptives and condoms but it seems for some natural is only good when it suits them or is not too inconvenient. Some try to live what they see as healthy life styles keeping fit and eating only good food yet smoke cannabis, take drugs like ecstasy and see no contradiction in what they do. Drugs like ecstasy are made with no or little controls and who knows what is put into these drugs as there is no quality control by qualified chemists and they are often made in houses with little concern for manufacturing hygiene. How blind we are at times. With so many anti-Christian values it is a great shame that some Christians support and vote for the Green parties when they promote such things. Of course it is good to support those who want to protect the planet and the people who live on it but if in doing so it means voting for sinful agendas then no Christian should do so otherwise they help sin to grow and become part of the reason for the spread of that which offends God.

Cardinal George Pell of Sydney Australia in an article on the August 8th 2010 said: "Many people, including myself, are concerned about the environment, so my second point was to urge my listeners to examine the policies of the Greens on their website and judge for themselves how thoroughly anti-Christian they are.

In 1996 the Green leader Bob Brown co-authored a short book *The Greens* with the notorious philosopher Peter Singer (now at Princeton University in U.S.A.) who rejects the unique status of humans and supports infanticide, as well as abortion and euthanasia.

They claimed humans are simply another smarter animal, so that humans and animals are on the same or similar levels depending on their level of consciousness. This Green ethic is designed to replace Judaeo-Christianity. Some Greens have taken this anti-Christian line further by claiming that, *no religious argumentation should be permitted in public debate* ... Naturally, the Greens are hostile to the notion of the family, man, woman and children, which they see as only one among a set of alternatives. They would allow marriage regardless of sexuality or gender identity ... For those who value our present way of life, the Greens are sweet camouflaged poison."

On 8th March 2011 the there was a report in The Australian newspaper: Tasmania is poised to become the first state to legalise voluntary euthanasia and to allow *death with dignity* clinics to operate.

Labor Premier Lara Giddings told The Australian late yesterday she was committed to working with the Greens to prepare a private member's bill for voluntary euthanasia.

Unfortunately, still some Catholics and Christians voted for the Greens and many still support them. How easy it is at times for people to be deceived and led away from God and to be led to accept what is totally against the will of God. Some political parties expect and demand that religion should play no part in politics and elections. Foolishly some Christians accept this view and do not realize that in doing so they deny their God. It is impossible for any true Christian not to let their faith decide whom they should vote for because their faith will and should be the driving force in their lives. Political parties with anti-Christian agendas cry the loudest using all sorts of false reasoning to get Christians to vote for them. Some even declare themselves more Christian than the Catholic Church hoping to get the Christian vote.

In August 2010 in Australia the Greens' leader Senator Bob Brown said that Cardinal George Pell's views do not represent mainstream Christian thinking, adding that the Greens' policies are closer to Christian ideals than the Cardinal's ideas. However, because many Christians have accepted over time the immorality and sinful ways of the world some believe statements like this to be true.

It is not only the greens in Australia with these immoral policies in England The Catholic Herald 28th April 2011 reports; The Green Party is backing calls for an end to the ban on same-sex marriage in the UK and in other EU member states.

Britain's two current Green MEPs – Caroline Lucas (South-East England) and Jean Lambert (London) – have said there should be marriage equality across the European Union.

Lucas said: "The Green Party is the only British political party that opposes the ban on same-sex civil marriage. We want marriage equality for LGBT couples."

She added: "It is time same-sex marriage was agreed and recognised by all EU member states. Lesbian and gay married couples should be able to move freely around Europe and have their marriages recognised on exactly the same basis as heterosexual married couples."

Or how about this? Greens are concerned that women seeking an abortion who can afford to "go private" can receive a swifter, and hence medically safer, procedure. The Greens want to abolish the current law that requires the consent of two doctors for an abortion. The Greens believe appropriately qualified midwives and nurses should be able to perform abortions, with the aim of improving access to NHS facilities. Currently women seeking an abortion face waits of up to seven weeks, and nearly 10% of abortions are carried out privately.

How is it possible for a Christian to remain Christian if they accept, support or vote for those promoting such evils as abortion, contraception, euthanasia, infanticide, embryonic stem cell research, homosexuality, gay adoption, living together in sin, same sex marriage, legalization of drugs of addiction and population control just to name a few? Those who declare themselves as Christian have to do their best to live to Christ's way otherwise they are Christian in name only. The world and its ways have corrupted the faith of many and continues to do so as people are led by the political parties with sinful agendas further and further away from God and the truth of His only Son, Jesus Christ.

The Solution

IT APPEARS THEN that from those early desires for change seeking a peaceful, just, loving and truly equal society evil has manipulated mankind and spread its cancer throughout the world. Evil has brought many to accept what is obviously wrong and to be blind to the truth. Evil has deceived mankind into believing it is walking the right path when in fact it walks the dark path of sin, suffering and pain. The search for the good society has brought a bad society as mankind has allowed its pride to rule its heart. The hope for a just society has led to an unjust one where those who seek to live to the truth of Jesus are persecuted. The hope for equality has led to an inequality where those who try to live to The Lord's way are at times not allowed to show their faith or symbols of it. The hope for a fairer society has led to a grossly unfair one where Christians can face prosecution for holding firm to their beliefs.

The hope for freedom of expression and of speech has led to a society where Christians are attacked if they express what are the truths of their faith. The hope for an end to discrimination has led to a society where Christians are discriminated against. The hope for a loving society has led to one that kills its own, young and old alike. The hope for a free society has led to one where many are slaves to their addictions. The hope for a harmonious society has led to one full of disharmony. What a mess we have made of the world and it seems we do not learn from our mistakes but just keep walking down the same path of selfishness, greed, immorality and the rejection of God.

Yet, through all this there is still the opportunity to change and to halt the slide into the realms of darkness. Mankind has a wonderful grace from God that within each heart is the seed of goodness and true love He has placed there. This grace has within it the power to overcome all evil and to stand firm against any assault of evil for God has put that power there. All it takes is for people to accept this grace by truly embracing The Lord, Jesus, and letting The Holy Spirit fill them through Him. Christians can, by the grace of God, bring the goodness and true love in the hearts of people to be alive and active as it is meant to be by bringing the others to know of Jesus' love for them and by encouraging others to accept the love and grace that Christ offers to all.

In this era there is the opportunity for Catholics to be like the early Church when people stood resolutely in the truth of Christ regardless of what the world or the evil in it may do to them. God has given each of His Son, Jesus' followers the chance to change the world as the early church did. However, we need to have the same determination as those Saints and Martyrs of days gone by. We, as they did, must declare ourselves openly for Christ. We must not be afraid to give our lives totally to and for Christ so that the power of His love can radiate through us and reverse the effects of evil in the world. As imitators of Christ, as His followers, we must not stand idly by and say we cannot do anything. Instead we must boldly, gently and lovingly proclaim the good news to all. This is our duty. This is what we are here for. If Christians want the world to be better they must work for it to be better. If Christians want morality to return they must live moral lives and reject all forms of immorality. If Christians want the leaders of countries to be honest, moral and good people then they must not vote for those who promote or accept the ways of evil. It is not acceptable to say that some of their policies are ok and that is what I voted for. If the political parties have immoral and sinful agendas the little good they do does not justify voting for them. It is time for Christians to speak out, to contact their political leaders in great numbers saying stop this immorality, stop this decay.

It is time for Christians to work together to show the world the right way to live, the right path to walk. Sadly within the Catholic Church at times there are divisions instead of unity. If the different groups within the Church worked together instead of opposing each other, which happens at times, the world would feel the effect of that united force of love. As I have travelled the world I have seen in places where different prayer groups seem to be fighting and opposing one another. I have seen where different movements condemn other movements within the Church even though the Church says they are valid. Some groups declare their way is the best way or the only way to truly follow Christ and His teachings regardless of what the Church has said about other movements. There are many ways of coming closer to God within the Catholic Church and each is a beautiful jewel bestowed from heaven. These movements and groups are gifts which are meant to be united so as to form a glittering crown of love and grace. The movements within the Church are supposed to be ones that show humility not pride, show love not bitterness and show that they accept God's will in the other devotions and ways He gives within the structure of the One Holy, Catholic and Apostolic Church. They are not meant to fight amongst one another. When they do so they make the evil one very happy for they weaken themselves and do not present to the world the love of God as they should.

It is also time for Christians to say *Enough* and start to demand firmly their rights but lovingly and without sin.

It is time for Christians to stand up and demand that Christian minorities in Muslim countries are given the same protections Muslim minorities in Christian countries and countries like Bosnia and the state of Kosovo receive.

In Saudi Arabia it is forbidden to have bibles, religious images and rosaries. If a Christian is caught wearing a cross any muslim can take it away. The person will be arrested, taken to prison and deported. There are cases in Saudi Arabia where converts to Christianity have been tortured and killed. It was reported in Zenit News about an Eritrean who converted to Christianity and spoke to others about Christ, who sits on death row because of this. Saudi Arabia is listed (Open Doors) as the 4th worst country where Christians are persecuted. Yet, many Christian leaders visit this country or deal with this country and remain silent about the terrible treatment of Christians there in case in doing so they might offend the Saudis whose oil, money, trade and strategic support seems more important than the rights and lives of Christians.

In the Ivory Coast recently an election was held and the muslim challenger won the election. Several countries in the west called for his opponent to step down and some western countries even gave limited military support. Yet, when a massacre of 800 Christians happened in a single day at the Catholic Mission of the Salesians, St. Teresa of the child Jesus in Duekoue, by the soldiers loyal to the muslim challenger, scant reporting and little protests were made.

Generally those who do stand up and speak out about the unjust treatment of Christians in the Muslim world are those of the churches which come under attack. In Iraq where the Christians suffer terribly and even a Catholic Archbishop, many priests and many Catholics have been murdered, very few Catholics in the west raise their voices in protest. As about 50% of Christians have been forced to leave their homeland of Iraq most Christians, most Catholics in the western world remain silent as this awful tragedy unfolds. I saw many Copts protesting around the world about the terrible attacks on them and their churches but how many Catholics stood with them? The Pope and the hierarchy spoke out but most Catholics did nothing and sat back in apathy instead of showing unity with their brothers and sisters of the Coptic Church. Catholics and Orthodox must stand together against this and all evil.

As Pope John Paul the 2nd explained the Eastern and Western parts of the Church are the two lungs of the Church and Pope Benedict the 16th reiterated this in 2007 with these words:

"Thank you, Your Beatitude, for this gesture of esteem and brotherly friendship. In you, I greet the Pastor of an ancient and illustrious Church, a shining tessera of that bright mosaic, the East, which, to use a favourite phrase of the Servant of God John Paul II of venerable memory, constitutes one of the two lungs with which the Church breathes."

Yes there are differences but we are together what makes the One Holy, Catholic and Apostolic Church and we must stand firmly together in the face of evil. It is time for Christians to go out united in the truth of Christ showing with humility that no longer will they accept the wrongs the world forces upon them. Now is the time for all of Christianity to raise its voice in love so that the influence of evil in the world can be confronted and overcome. If Catholics and Christians do this then the world will change, all it takes is for each one who loves Jesus to say *Yes* and to truly be His followers.

The Pillars of Faith

THE POWER TO stand firm in Christ, Our Lord's love and truth is offered to each one in the pillars of faith that He gives to us in the Sacraments, in the unadulterated Holy Word of God, in prayer, in obedience and in sacrificing.

In the Sacraments God offers Himself, His love and His grace and nothing can stand against these or the person who truly lives in them and for them. In the Sacraments God is there for us to lean on when we feel weak, to rely upon when we are uncertain and to shelter in when we are under attack.

In the Holy Word of God, Jesus shows and explains to each one how to stand against the evil in the world and that is to live as He lived and to live to what He said to us as He said it and meant it. Not how some people interpret it in their worldly ways or selective ways in their acceptance of His word.

March 11th 2011 Pope Benedict the 16th also called on priests today not to shrink from proclaiming "the entire plan of God." "This is important," said the Pope. "The Apostle does not preach Christianity *a la carte*, according to his own tastes, he does not preach a Gospel according to his own preferred theological ideas; he does not take away from the commitment to announce the entire will of God, even when uncomfortable, nor the themes he may least like personally."

Prayer, which when said in love and a true desire to be a follower of The Lord, opens the soul to the gifts and graces needed. Prayer which strengthens, as it brings the person's focus away from self and onto God and increases the desire for doing only His will.

In obedience to the One Holy, Catholic and Apostolic Church which is the body of Christ and which when speaks is Christ, Himself, speaking to mankind. Obedience is hated by evil for the evil one is the prince of disobedience and tries to bring all to disobedience. When a person is totally obedient to God and His Holy, Catholic Church the evil one squirms in anguish as the Light of Our Divine Lord fills the obedient one and pours out through them to the world around. It is in obedience that a person can face the evil in the world and show truly they are in love with God and desire only to serve Him.

In sacrificing, Catholics are called to carry the cross with Christ. Just as Our Lord carried the cross in love of mankind so we too must be prepared to carry not only our own crosses but also the crosses of those who cannot or will not carry them. It is in doing so others can come not only to see the love of Christ in us but can also experience His love in our actions. The evil in the world calls people to think of self so we must do the opposite, we must think of others before ourselves. In doing so we are filled with grace by The Holy Spirit and are strengthened in our faith. In doing so we can humble ourselves before all, just as Our Lord did, and without pride truly become the saints the world needs today. In doing so we become vessels through which The Lord can work to bless the world and to heal mankind. It is in sacrificing we can imitate the early Church and be like those brave men and women who gave their all for the love of Christ and for the love of others.

Catholics are the ones chosen by God to bring the fullness of His love and truth to all. Catholics are chosen by God to be the lights of Christ's love that disperse the darkness of evil in the world. Catholics are chosen to be the ones who will not bow before evil but will stand erect with heads held high clinging to the victory of Christ over evil and proclaiming that victory to all. Catholics are chosen by God to be the lambs of love that brings the world back to its senses and back into the way of life that is the holy way, the loving way and the best way; the way of Christ.

Let each Catholic become a pillar of faith themselves unmovable in their belief and unshakable in their love of God. Now is the time to stop the rotten stench and decay of evil that has spread throughout society and replace it with the sweet fragrance of the love of God. Let each Catholic go out and reap a rich harvest for The Lord. Do not say someone else can or will do it, say, *I will do it*. Catholics should not ignore their responsibility to the future generations, the responsibility of leaving them a good and holy world to live in. All it takes is for brave Catholics to stand for Christ and to stand against the world and then the future in Christ, Our Lord, will be a glorious one. The people of the One Holy, Catholic and Apostolic Church should know and believe the power of God is with them, for in truth it is. The people of the One Holy, Catholic and Apostolic Church should know that Christ, Our Lord is standing with them and that they are not alone, for in truth He is. In this knowledge the people of the One Holy, Catholic and Apostolic Church should go out and grasp this opportunity to change lives, to save souls and to be the saints history will look back upon and say truly these were followers of Christ.

Interview

AN INTERVIEW WITH Alan Ames by Beatrix Zureich
June 2009

BZ: Before your conversion in 1992, your life seemed to be very successful – you had a high paying job and were the captain of the Australian National Team in Aikido (martial arts). When heaven came to you, asking you to change your life, you didn't easily give in. Were you afraid of the change heaven wanted or were you happy with life as it was and didn't see a need of change?

AA: At first I was uncertain as to what was happening but once I was certain it was heaven communicating with me I wanted to change. All the things of the world I had became of little value to me as I only now wanted to please God so the worldly things had no hold on me. I was not afraid of the change heaven wanted but I was unsure if I was capable of changing but the Lord told me He would give me the grace I needed to change if I truly wanted it.

BZ: Upon hearing your story, some people say, why should we listen to him? Who knows if his story is true … There are so many visionaries and prophets today, it's too hard to find out the authentic ones …

AA: First I say to people it is the Catholic Church and it's teachings that people should listen to and follow. If anything I say or do goes against Church teaching they should ignore or reject it. As they should with all others regardless of what they say is happening in their lives i.e. God speaking to them, Mary, our mother speaking to them. I also say to people that if anyone does not accept the authority of the Catholic Church or say they do not need it because they are ecumenical do not listen to them. Obedience is a clear sign of what is happening in a person's life and we should remember the prince of disobedience, the one who was first disobedient to God was Lucifer and in disobedience we follow Lucifer's example. The Catholic Church is the Body of Christ and we must be obedient to it.

It is up to each person to decide if they believe in my words or not but I suggest they read or listen to them before they make any judgement. I only say what I know to be true (some of which has been witnessed and testified to by others) and I hope that in my experiences that maybe some others in need will find some of the help they may need.

BZ: It seems the whole world is in search of love, looking for it in many places. God is love. Why would not all find His love? Does every soul get their chance to find God?

AA: It is true all have a desire for true love deep inside, it is a God given desire that is meant to lead each person to the love of God and of each other. God gives each person opportunities throughout their life to grow in this desire of true love. Some accept these opportunities and in their lives this is seen by the good lives they lead in love of God and in love of others. Sadly, many others put the false love that is self centered and of the world first in their lives and so deny themselves the grace to find God's love. It is in false love that a person closes their heart to true love and opens it to sin. Love of self is of course pride. While love of worldly things is only a reflection of that pride as a person seeks for themselves in this life the pleasures of the world. Through this pride the person become a denier of God and an embracer of evil. This pride brings a blindness that allows evil to grow and that effect of pride can be seen so clearly today. Now greed, gluttony, lust, selfishness, disrespect of the value of life, hatred and other sinful ways swamp the world and many people see no wrong in them, many embrace them and become part of them.

Incredibly then some of these people blame God for the problems in the world. Wondering why He does not fix them not seeing they are part of the problem and that they need to fix their lives first if they want the world's problems to be solved.

God said to mankind from the beginning that if we live to His way of love the world will be a paradise. We do not live as God asks and so we create a world full of suffering in our rejection of God's loving will.

BZ: How is your relationship with the Church and what is obedience for you?

AA: I hope I have the relationship all should have with the Catholic Church; I love it. How can I not for it is the body of Christ? Within His body Christ offers me His love and the way to heaven. He offers Himself in the Eucharist, He offers me forgiveness in reconciliation and He offers me divine grace in and through all the Sacraments.

Because I love God and I love His Church, I desire to be obedient to the Catholic Church as I know God's will is seen in it and heard from it.

To me obedience is a cornerstone of our faith and I see how important it is that all Catholics are obedient to the church if they truly want to live their faith in true love of God.

BZ: Some people have suffered terribly in life and have been hurt by others. How can we help them to come to God and trust Him?

AA: There are many who suffer some of whom turn away from God in their suffering maybe thinking, "If there was a God He would not let me suffer so." Some think God would not let others hurt them and when others do then God is rejected. These thoughts come in the times of weakness when a person may be vulnerable to the doubts that evil tries to put into their minds. If the person succumbs to these doubts then they can remain with them for a long time.

To help people overcome these thoughts and beliefs it is important we show a compassionate love that does not condemn the people for their doubts or does not try to force them back to God. We should try, through gentle understanding and encouraging love, to help them reach out to God. Explaining to them that these thoughts in themselves can cause pain in life as turmoil grows within the person. Turmoil which can turn into anger, hatred and bitterness transforming the person into someone they were not before, someone who now may cause others they love hurt through their words and actions. It is important to gently bring their focus on to the suffering of Our Lord, Jesus, if it is possible to do so, and explain how

He suffered more than they did but that The Lord never blamed God or felt angry towards the Father or others. He endured in forgiving love offering all to the Father so that others may come to know His love. How through His suffering the depth and strength of His love was seen and how this can be the same with them. How through their hurt if they show love, that others will benefit and not be hurt from them doing so and the love others have for them will be strengthened and grow. It is a cheerful heart that brings joy to others and when a person is cheerful not miserable in their suffering the grace that is poured out is very powerful in the lives of those they come in contact. Also with the showing of love through their pain and hurt the love comforts the person themselves within soothing their heart as it flows through it.

Before any of this is done though it is important we first pray to the Holy Spirit for the grace to speak the right words in the right way and to truly be examples of God's love. Examples that do not get angry if they are shouted at or abused. Examples that do not turn away when a person becomes difficult. Examples that always show a loving heart no matter what happens. Doing so is often what opens the hearts of those suffering to God as they see the love of God in you. This may take some time and it may be difficult but we should expect that and pray for the patient love to endure.

BZ: You have dedicated your life to spreading God's love and that involves a lot of travelling. Isn't it hard to be on planes for so many hours, to eat different foods, to risk your health or even your life?

AA: By the grace of God I am blessed to travel to many places to spread the love of God and I thank Him for permitting me to do this. Yes, it is very hard at times and I do not like travelling but without it the work would not get done. It is hard being away from home and I miss my wife very much. The foods at times do not agree with me and my health suffers because I am a diabetic and it can be hard to control it. Yes, my life has been at risk. However, should I expect it to be any different? The Lord, Jesus, suffered and as His follower I cannot expect that I will not. There are many who have suffered for the Lord so why should I be any different? The Lord said to me from the beginning it would not be easy and, even though I did not imagine it would be as hard as it is, I accept that. The wonderful thing is that God gives me the grace and the strength I need to do His will and He fills me with joy even in the most difficult times.

It is only by God's grace I can continue and as long as He gives me that grace I will carry on doing as He asks. I think often of what St. Teresa of Avilla said to me, "In me my weakness, in God my strength." That helps me remember it is God's loving strength I rely on and not myself.

BZ: Some people say, "If I had the Lord speaking to me, I would be a better person, I could ask Him what to do in life and He would save me from making mistakes." Do you think it is easier for you to live a good life than it is for others?

AA: Maybe it is but I do not ask God what I should do in my life as I believe He will tell me anything I need to know and so there is no need to ask but a need to trust. I still make mistakes because I have my free will and sometimes in my weakness I do my will instead of God's. However as soon as I recognise this I beg the Lord to help me do only

His will and to forgive me for my mistakes. God offers all guidance to do His will in The Commandments, the life of The Lord, Jesus, and the teachings of the Catholic Church and if people, including myself, follow those then we know what to do in life and as for being a better person we all can be better by living to those.

BZ: There are people who are very desperate in their lives, and they would do anything to get the least sign of God, to hear or see or feel that they are not alone, that God is there for them. What is your advice for them?

AA: Go to the Eucharist in adoration and in the Holy Mass and allow The Lord, Jesus, to fill you with His divine presence and grace. Open your hearts in love to Our Eucharistic Lord and ask Him to let you feel a touch of His love. Doing this and focusing totally on God as you do so and persevering in doing so will bring you to experience Him in an intimate way. Once that happens never again does a person feel alone as they know God is with them loving them.

BZ: Do you encourage prayers for the poor souls, for those who passed away?

AA: Of course this is an important part of our faith. I pray for all the departed no matter who they are or what they have done hoping God will be merciful to them all. In the Holy Mass all the departed, all those who have died, are prayed for so if it is in the Sacrament of Sacraments this should be in my prayers too. Surely as a follower of Jesus a person should have the desire that all will be saved, even though this may not be so.

I discovered when I fell in love with Jesus that I also had this burning desire that all would experience mercy in Him. I want no one to suffer in Hell and I want all to be in heaven with The Lord. I want all the sinners to find mercy in Him and salvation in Him. It hurts me deeply to think that some will suffer eternally, that some will not see heaven and so I pray that the mercy of God will be shown. I do not understand His mercy and I know it is fathomless so my hope is in that Divine Mercy just as we pray, "bring all souls to heaven especially those in most need of your mercy."

BZ: You have the gift of healing, many healings are reported worldwide after your praying over people. Does God want to heal everyone or is healing only for a selected few?

AA: God offers all healing in His divine love but always it is up to the person to accept what God offers. Sometimes people deny healing because they are not prepared to change their lives in the way needed for the healing to occur. This change may be to stop doing or accepting sin in their lives. It may be to come to church more, to receive the sacraments more, to pray more or to focus more on heaven than on earth. Sadly some will not do what is needed for the healing to happen and so deny themselves healing.

In Holy Scripture Jesus sometimes called for an act of faith for the healing to happen. To one man He said, "Pick up your bed and walk." In an act of faith the man did it and was healed. Jesus also said to some who were healed, "Go and sin no more." So we can see He was asking people to play their part in the healing with acts of faith and with rejection of sin. Today it is the same He calls us to play our part and when we do often this is when the healing happens.

BZ: Many in the West are attracted to Buddhism, especially after meeting the Dalai Lama.

AA: People sometimes look to eastern mysticism seeking the answers for life not realising all the answers can be found in the Catholic Church. Often the nice sounding messages of eastern beliefs are attractive because people do not look fully to what is being said or because people have problems living to Jesus' way and look for an easier way. However, often they do not recognise that these ways are frequently self-centered ways which are about the person improving themselves and bringing the focus on self and away from God. Suggesting that a person can reach higher levels until one day they reach a divine state. This in itself is a denial of God. Some say there are many gods i.e. Monkey god, Elephant god etc. Again this is a denial of the one true God and also a lowering of the value of humanity. Some say we come back reincarnated as various animals again this is a devaluing of humanity by placing it on the same level as animals. It is also a denial of the true and eternal life The Lord, Jesus, offers people in Him. In some of these beliefs there is little mention of sacrificing for others it is about self. It is important that people understand when they look to these ways they truly are looking away from and denying the truth of God, Jesus Christ.

BZ: We thank you for the interview and please include us and everyone who reads this in your prayers. God bless you.

Messages

As you read the messages you will see some have scriptural references while others have none. This is because The Lord at times gives me references while at other times He does not. When I am given a reference from Holy Scripture it may be one or two lines or only one or two words from a line. Sometimes two or three lines from different parts of Holy Scripture are combined to make the reference. The references were at first either taken from the Jerusalem or the Douay-Rheims Bibles but later to avoid any confusion my spiritual director Fr. Gerard Dickinson and I agreed to only use the New American Bible for references.

Angels

St. Gabriel (Archangel)
Angels on high look to helping mankind find their true place in heaven. Angels on high hold no jealousy towards mankind only a desire for mankind to find their home in heaven. Angels on high are pleased to do and accept God's will for mankind for in doing so the angels know they please God.
Revelations 7:11 all the angels. | *1 Thessalonians 5:18 of God.*

St. Gabriel (Archangel)
>Angelic love is a gift of God.

Jesus
>In heaven My throne is surrounded by angels constantly singing of their love for Me. United with the angels in this chorus of love are the saints in heavenly glory. Still there is enough room for all of mankind to come and join in this joyful choir and I hope all will accept their invitation, for I long to hear each one singing in love to Me.
>*Psalm 103:19 the lord's throne.*

St. Michael (Archangel)
>By your side is an angel God has sent to protect you.
>By your side is an angel God has sent to care for your soul.
>By your side is an angel who loves you;
>An angel who is God's gift to you and an angel who sees you as God's gift to Him.

St. Michael (Archangel)
>An angel's breath you may not feel but know
>that the angels are real.

A Pilgrimage

God the Father
>If you live each day as a pilgrimage seeking My love then you will find each day brings you closer to Me and closer to your final destination of heaven.

Beautiful Gifts

Jesus

As the sun was setting a man looked at the sky and said to himself, "What a beautiful sunset." Then he sat down thinking on the sight before him and how nothing mankind made compared to the beauty he was now seeing. Then in a moment it came to him that whoever created such beauty must have a beautiful heart from which it came. Then he realized that of course it was God who had created the sunset and that God must have a beautiful heart. As this thought continued he came to realize that God must be true beauty and that God must be the creator of all that is beautiful. Then in his mind he saw all the different peoples of the world and came to understand that God had created them all and that being so all people must be beautiful. At that moment he stood up and reached to his sleeve to tear off the swastika that was on it, saying out loud, "How can I hate anyone for all are beautiful gifts of God's love."

He decided there and then that no longer would he listen to the words of hate from his leaders and no longer would he see anyone regardless of race as less than him. The man walked home smiling and feeling a peace within him. A peace that would carry him through the torture and death that lay ahead of him for rejecting the creed of his SS masters. A peace that would bring him to God's glory in heaven through his martyrdom.

St. Bartholomew

There is a beauty in every person.
There is a masterpiece in everyone.
There is a unique splendour in every heart.
This is there because God in His love created them all.

Jesus
> To look upon another and to say they are ugly is a rejection of the beautiful God-given gift in each person.

Children

Jesus
> Treat children with love, for they need to be loved.

Jesus
> The innocent heart of a child is an example of how all people should be regardless of age.

Confusion

Jesus
> There is confusion where sin abounds.
> There is confusion where evil is strong.
> There is confusion where wrong tries to overcome what is right.
> Be aware of why confusion is often there.
> *2 Corinthians 2:11 so that we may not be taken advantage of by satan.*

Creation

God the Father
> Nature is the gift of creation in action, an action I have formed and an action that is designed for all to live in harmony within. Mankind needs to be careful not to damage this system that I have created or it risks damaging itself.
> *1 John 2:16 all that is in the world.*

St. Francis of Assisi
>In creation is God's love, do not be blind to it
>and do not treat creation with contempt.

Jesus
>In nature see the power of the Father's creative love.
>*Sirach 3:9 father's blessing.*

Darkness

St. Thomas Aquinas
>The prince of darkness is like a grain of dirt beneath
>your shoe when you trust completely in God and are
>obedient to His will.

God the Father
>The day dawns, the Son rises, the darkness leaves.
>The day My Son, Jesus rose from the dead, the darkness
>was illuminated with the light of His victorious love.
>This is the day all should rise to leaving the darkness
>behind as they embrace My Son, Jesus in love.

Death

St. Peter Chanel
>In death God's glory can be seen
>if you remain steadfast in your faith.

Jesus
>With every breath love Me and know when you
>take your last one you will come to My eternal love.

Disagreements

Jesus
> When people argue it can open them to anger and hatred so any disagreements should be faced in kindness and in love to avoid the risk of being drawn into sin.
> *Psalm 36:11 continue your kindness towards your friends, your just defense of the honest heart.*

Jesus
> When you feel an argument is about to begin take care to show love so as to avoid it.

Easter Time

Jesus
> All the pain and all the suffering from all the sins of mankind I took onto My heart and offered each person the opportunity to be set free in Me.

Jesus
> My sacrifice on the cross was finite and yet infinite; a divine mystery. The moment of My death was one moment in time and yet it spanned eternity; a divine grace. My words of forgiving love from the cross were words that begun and ended in the sentence I spoke, yet those same words exist eternally; a divine revelation.
> Time exists in God and yet God came and lived in time revealing to mankind a divine mystery that in God's grace what seems impossible becomes possible.

God the Father
>In the tomb My Son Jesus showed that in death is but the doorway to heaven for those who believe in Him.
>In the tomb My Son Jesus showed that in death hell had no grip on those who loved Him.
>In the tomb My Son Jesus showed that in death His glory shone brightly and for those who died in His love they would be glorified in Him.
>*1 Timothy 1:11 the glorious.*
>*Romans 9:30 those he justified he also glorified.*

God the Father
>After suffering and dying for the love of man, My Son, Jesus rested before rising in glory to bring the love of God into hearts that are nothing but empty tombs without His love in them.

God the Father
>From the tomb the peace of My Son, Jesus reached into the turmoil of hell and brought His light into the darkness.
>*2 Thessalonians 3:16 the Lord of peace.*

God the Father
>Placing yourself beside My Son, Jesus as He lay in the tomb will bring you eternal peace, as you will come to know that Jesus is the master of death and that death could not master Him.
>*John 19:11 Jesus answered, "You will have no power over me."*

God the Father
> While My Son, Jesus lay resting in the tomb
> angels all around Him filled the room.
> Each angel knelt in silent prayer
> paying homage to evil's slayer.
> These angelic hearts reached out in love
> to the King Who had lived on earth below
> but came from heaven above.
> As this heavenly chorus united in silent worship
> they prayed in the hope that all mankind
> would accept My Son Jesus' kingship.
> Today the angels still make this call
> and hope that My Son,
> Jesus will be recognized as King by all.
> *Psalm 47:8 king over all the earth.*

God the Father
> This time between My Son's death and resurrection is a time to meditate on the way My Son Jesus died in love and the way He arose in love, Showing in death and in life the importance of loving God and showing for those who do so that they too will arise to live in His eternal love.

God the Father
> By His cross My Son, Jesus, defeated evil.
> By His resurrection My Son, Jesus, defeated death.

Jesus
> In three days the power of My love
> was shown to the world. The power that saves.
> The power that raises the lowly on high.
> The power that is denied to none who seek it
> with a true heart. The power of God.
> *Job 23:6 his great power*
> *1 Corinthians 1:24 Christ, the power of God*

God the Father
> Today My Son, Jesus, arose bringing hope for all people. Hope that in Him all can be raised to live eternally in heaven.
> *Colossians 1:5 the hope reserved for you in heaven*

God the Father
> With My Son's resurrection the fear of death for those who love Him should be dispelled.

Jesus
> In My resurrection all people can find security and peace.
> In My resurrection all people can find the key to heaven.
> In My resurrection all people can find the truth that will set them free if they believe in Me.
> *1 Thessolonians 4:14 if we believe that Jesus died and rose*

Jesus
> Death cannot hold those who imitate Me. Death cannot corrupt those who live for Me. Death cannot stop those who are faithful rising in My glory.
> This is the truth of My resurrection, the resurrection all are called to be part of.
> *Matthew 28:7 raised from the dead.*

Emptiness

Jesus

> Life for many today is empty because they do not know My love. It is only in Me that life can truly be fulfilled and it is only in Me the emptiness will truly disappear.

Enjoyment

Jesus

> To enjoy oneself should not be at the expense of others. If it is then joy is not what people will find, but only misery. Misery for the one whose expense it is at and misery for the one who thinks they have found joy at the expense of others for in the end they will have to answer for the wrong they do.

Error

God the Father

> If a person lives in error it is impossible for them to know the fullness of truth.

Equality

God the Father

> There should be no class distinction among people for in My eyes all are equal. Anyone who believes different will find themselves full of shame and suffering when they come to stand before My Son, Jesus on judgment day.

Eternal Life

God the Father
　　I breathe my love into every soul that is created. My breath which can bring eternal life to those who live recognizing the gift I have given or which, for those who reject or deny My loving breath, will bring suffocation to their soul.

Family

Jesus
　　The love between parents and children should be a reflection of My Father's love for mankind.

God the Father
　　Every father who loves their children should try to help their children to reach their full potential and have a happy life. In that way their fatherhood becomes a reflection of Mine.
　　Proverbs 10:1 his father.

St. Joseph
　　My family was made holy with God as part of it. So it can be with all families that make God part of their family.

Jesus
　　As a parent it is natural to want to protect your children from harm. As part of the family of mankind you should feel this way towards all people.

Jesus
> A family reunion occurs every time
> someone comes back to Me.

St. Paul
> It is in the love of God you become family to all people.
> It is in pride you become isolated in self.

God the Father
> Families may argue at times but at no time should it be forgotten that they are family and that they should be united in love. Mankind, My family of love.

St. Joseph
> All people are called to be part of God's family.
> How sad it is that many see no reason to answer that call.

FEAR

St. Sebastian
> Those who fear are weak, those who trust in God are strong.

St. Peter
> As Jesus hung on the cross calling out to mankind I love you many of His followers ran and hid in fear. I was one of those. As Jesus resurrected He called out to mankind there is nothing to fear, come to life in Me. Many of His followers listened to His words and accepted His grace and strength into their lives not fearing again. I was one of those. Today Jesus is still calling people to life in Him, our resurrected Lord and I join His call saying to people become one of those like me.
> *1 Peter 2:4 come to him.*

Jesus
> If you live in My truth you have nothing to fear.
> It is when you live outside of it you do.

God the Father
> With so many fears in the world no wonder peace is elusive.
> Peace will come to earth when mankind places its trust in
> My Son, Jesus and stops being afraid.

Jesus
> Do not be afraid be strong in trust of Me.
> Do not be afraid be strong in love of Me.
> Do not be afraid be strong in Me.
> *Jeremiah 46:28 never fear, says the lord, for I am with you*

God the Father
> When the fear of the world takes hold of a person
> then the way of evil taking hold of them is opened.
> *Isaiah 51:7 fear not*

God the Father
> Time can be like a cross if a person lets their fears take hold
> or it can be like a joyful gift if they let My love take hold.

Jesus
> If you fear evil it can destroy you,
> if you trust in Me it cannot.

Following the Lord

St. Andrew
> Following the Lord, Jesus, should be a love and joy filled
> experience it is self that may stop it being so.

St. Andrew
>To proclaim God's love to the world is the duty of all who follow His Son and our Lord, Jesus. A duty some deny and in doing so deny others the opportunity of knowing the complete love of God.

Freedom of Choice

Jesus
>I see the good in people and how in My love it can grow if the person makes the right decisions in their lives. Then I give them every opportunity and a helping hand to guide them towards the right decision, but in doing so I still allow them the freedom of choice.
>
>Freedom given in love with the hope that in the free choice of love each person will grow to reach their full potential in life.

God the Father
>The will to love Me is your free choice.
>The desire to love Me is a result of that choice.
>The reward of living eternally in My love
>comes from your free choice and from the desire
>to love Me above all others including self.

Gentle

Jesus
>The gentle imitate Me.

Gifts

Jesus
>The most important gift you can give to anyone
is My love wrapped in yours.

God the Father
>When you hear a bird sing remember it is a gift of My love.
When you hear a bird sing know that each note is
praising Me. When you hear a bird sing understand that
its song is one of love created by Me.

God the Father
>All the gifts I offer to mankind are offered in My love
and if mankind accepts them in love then the gifts will
reach their full potential.

Glory

Jesus
>It is when a person loves Me completely
they come to see the glory of God in all of creation.
Psalm 103:22 everywhere in God's domain.

God the Father
>The glory of My love fills each moment and it is when
a person tries to live each moment in My love that My
glory is seen in them.

Jesus
>When your last moment on earth comes, if it is a
moment given to Me in love, it will be a moment that
leads you to eternal glory.

Good and Evil

God the Father

An evil person is one who gives themselves knowingly and willingly to the dark. All others are just confused people who need help to avoid being ensnared by the evil they at times accept into their lives.

God the Father

Throughout the history of mankind there has been a battle between good and evil. Mankind in its foolishness keeps the battle alive instead of accepting and embracing the victory of My Son, Jesus Who, from the cross, won the war.

God the Father

Sometimes the evil in the world makes people do things that under other circumstances they would not do. This is how evil works, making good people confused and then leading them into committing sin that should be rejected by them. Evil sows confusion and in confusion sin slips in, often unnoticed.

God the Father

Good people at times do bad things but that does not necessarily make them bad. It just means they are weak and need help in overcoming their weaknesses.

St. Stanislaus
Facing tyranny, facing evil, facing what is wrong. It is the duty of all Christians to stand firm in their faith opposing wrong and denying evil when they face it, showing the love of God in all situations and showing that God will forgive even the worst tyrant if they repent.
Sirach 5:6 he will forgive.

St. Stanislaus
There is nothing to fear from evil if your faith is strong.
Sirach 3:9 firm.
Sirach 2:2 steadfast, undisturbed in times of adversity.

St. Paul of the cross
As Christ, Our Lord, suffered and died evil thought it was winning. When the Lord arose evil saw it was not so but in its pride evil closed its eyes to the truth. The evil that was in the lives of those who persecuted the Lord in His life on earth and the evil that is in the lives of those who persecute His followers and in the lives of those who deny His loving victory today.

God the Father
Bad thoughts of others can soon lead people deeper into sin. It is always wise to think good and in that way be led deeper into good.

Jesus
Over all the world evil tries to spread its blanket of sin and sadly some people pull this blanket over themselves willingly, believing it will bring them the warmth of wealth and security when in fact all it will bring is the coldness of suffering and pain.

Hearts

St. Thomas Aquinas

All the might in the world cannot stand against the power of God's love in your heart if you have faith in His power.
Romans 12:21 do not be conquered by evil but conquer evil with good.

Jesus

A heart totally obedient to My will is one that will reach heaven. This is a guarantee I give and it is one that will be fulfilled.

Jesus

Hearts that love Me are sweet smelling roses.
Hearts that hate Me are foul smelling weeds.
The roses will be collected and together will make a beautiful fragrance that will be eternal.
While the weeds will be collected and burned giving off an acrid odour that will feed its own flames forever.
Ezekiel 15:7 the fire shall devour them.

Jesus

A loving heart, a patient heart, a forgiving heart,
an obedient heart, a giving heart, a serving heart,
a humble heart, a truthful heart, a compassionate heart
is the heart I want all my followers to have.
John 1:37 followed Jesus.

Jesus

From the heart comes love,
it is only the mind and the will that stops this being so.
Proverbs 25:20 the human heart.

Jesus
>With every heartbeat remember it is a gift
>of My Father's love for you.

Jesus
>The first thing that should be in the heart of all people
>is to love God. The second is to love each other as I have
>loved you. The hearts that do this are the ones that can
>truly be called Christian and can truly be called holy.

God the Father
>With each moment of life on earth comes a grace for
>every person. The grace to live in My love and be happy.
>All it takes is a person accepting this grace into their
>heart and believing in the love I offer them.

God the Father
>In each heart there is a longing to be loved and to love.
>That longing can only be satisfied in My love, for it is in
>My love hearts are filled and hearts can grow to become
>ones that truly are satisfied.

God the Father
>The fragrance that comes from the heart that loves is
>a joy to Me. The stench that comes from the heart that
>sins is a sadness to Me. Bring Me joy by loving in all
>situations.

St. Patrick
>I brought the heart of the Irish to God
>and this I pray is where it will remain.

Jesus
> When your heart is one in Mine you will find sanctity.
> *Proverbs 16:1 in his heart.*

Jesus
> Within the heart of a priest must be a home for the heart of God to reside in if the priesthood is to be lived to its full potential.

Jesus
> A bitter heart may not only break itself
> but it may break many other hearts too.

Jesus
> There is love in every heart when it is created. Love which should be nurtured so that the person can grow to be an image of love in their life. I AM that love and in My love each person can become an image of Me to others.

Jesus
> In every heart there should be love for Me
> as in My heart there is love for every heart.

Jesus
> As a heart beats in love for Me
> each beat becomes grace- filled to help that love grow.

Jesus
> When My spirit touches a heart
> emotions of love are unchained.

Jesus
>An indifferent heart is one open to evil,
>a loving heart is one open to Me.

God the Father
>Under the influence of drugs hearts are open to sin.
>Under the influence of My Holy Spirit hearts are open to love. Sadly, many people make the wrong choice and sadly many hearts are hurt because they do.

Jesus
>With a kind word you can change a heart.
>With a forgiving word you can mend a broken heart.
>With a loving word you can fill a lonely heart.
>The word that is My Word.

Heaven

God the Father
>It does not matter what nationality a person may be,
>all are called to be citizens of heaven.

Jesus
>In heaven there are no nationalities,
>only saints and angels in love with Me.

Jesus
>The grace of My love is enough to lift all of mankind to heaven if only mankind accepts and embraces the love I offer.

Jesus
> It will be a great day of celebration in heaven
> when mankind finally accepts Me as Lord.

Helping Others

Jesus
> Support those in need.
> Help those who struggle.
> Aid those with difficulties,
> And do it all because you love Me.

Jesus
> It is the duty of all who walk with Me
> to encourage others to join them in their walk.
> *Tobit 13:13 together.*

Holiness

St. Anthony of Padua
> To find holiness one only needs to live in the Sacraments,
> for in doing so you live in God Who is holiness itself.

Holy Scripture

God the Father
> The words of Holy Scripture are there to guide you home to heaven. The words of Holy Scripture are there to guide you to live a happy and fulfilled life. The words of Holy Scripture are there as a gift of My love to mankind. A gift that needs to be read and accepted in love to truly understand what is in each word; I AM.
> *Proverbs 29:26 each are from the Lord.*

Humour

God the Father
People often do not know what they are doing or the price they will have to pay when people make fun of My Son, Jesus. Pray for them to see their blasphemy for what it is; a doorway that can lead to hell.

Joy

God the Father
If every person was to call to Me in love, they would be filled in return with My joy and the world would change to become the joy filled gift of My love that it was created to be.
Sirach 37:24 full enjoyment.

God the Father
The joy a person feels when they know a loved one is safe is miniscule in comparison to the joy I have each time a soul comes to heaven.

Knowledge

St. Bede
All knowledge should centre on God otherwise it is an empty knowledge.

St. Bede
To teach a soul to love God is the greatest lesson one can give.

St. Bede
>In knowledge may be power but in God is the almighty.
>*Wisdom 12:18 master of might.*

St. Andrew the Apostle
>Peace comes with knowing and loving God for Our Lord, Jesus, is the prince of peace.

St. Andrew the Apostle
>The greatest teacher ever is our Lord and God, Jesus Christ, and all people should listen to Him and learn from Him if they seek true knowledge and true love.

Life

God the Father
>Without love a life is empty.
>Without hope a life is one of despair.
>Without faith a life is a meaningless one.
>My Son, Jesus, is the faithful love that all should hope in if they seek a life with meaning.
>*Sirach 51:1 refuge of my life.*

Jesus
>Today live for Me and tomorrow you will be with Me forever.

St. Leo the Great
>A Christian life must be by its very nature one of crosses, one of sacrifices and one of love.

God the Father
>In the life of each person is My love.
>In the life of each person is My grace.
>In the life of each person is My gift.
>Sadly, so many are blind to this and do not appreciate what I have given in each life.

St. Cyril
>In the lives of those who sin is the risk of eternal death.

St. Thomas the Apostle
>The most important reason for living should be to love God for it is from His love you came and by His grace that hopefully to His love you will return.
>*John 20:10 returned home.*

LOST SOULS

Holy Spirit
>Throughout the world are many lost souls, many drooping spirits and many broken hearts; results of mankind turning away from Me. The heart of mankind needs to change now so that My spirit of love will fill their souls and bring them to the joy-filled life each one was created to live.
>*1 Corinthians 10:33 the many, that they may be saved.*

St. Theodosius
>To guide a lost soul to God is one of the greatest acts of love a person can do for another.

Love

Jesus
> It is better to love than to hate for in love there is peace whereas in hatred there is only turmoil.

God the Father
> My love for mankind began before I created man.
> My love for mankind exists in every moment.
> My love for mankind will never end.
> *Thessalonians 1:4 loved by God.*

Jesus
> I look upon each person and love them, and all I ask in return is that they look to Me in love.

Jesus
> Every life can be one filled with love
> if each person turns to Me and seeks to live in My love.

God the Father
> The fruit of love is more love.

Jesus
> The only impression you should make is one of love.

Jesus
> Love is a greater treasure than wealth.

God the Father
> In love there is only goodness,
> otherwise it truly is not love.

Jesus
>If others do not love you it should not stop you loving them.

Jesus
>A heart of love is the heart I desire My followers to have.
>*Romans 8:28 those who love God.*

Jesus
>To imitate Me the person must love all people in all situations and with no regard to standing within society.

Making the Effort

God the Father
>It is wise to make the effort needed to love those you find it hard to relate to for more often than not they need to be loved.

Marriage

God the Father
>One man, one woman united in love in one holy marriage is the way marriage is meant to be. Any other form of marriage is wrong and brings only sin into the lives of those who partake of them. Marriage is for life. Marriage is a holy Sacrament. Marriage is a promise to God that cannot be broken unless it truly was not a marriage. Marriage without that promise to Me is not a marriage at all.
>*Malachi 2:16 for I hate divorce says the Lord, God of Israel.*

Jesus

Love between a husband and wife is sacred and no one should break that love for in doing so they run the risk of eternal damnation.
Matthew 5:27 you shall not commit adultery.
Matthew 5:32 whoever divorces his wife causes her to commit adultery and whoever marries a divorced woman commits adultery.

God the Father

It was early in the morning when the man awoke and could not get back to sleep. He lay there trying not to move too much so as not to disturb his sleeping wife. He turned to look at her and smiled as he thought how happy she had made him in their married life. He thought of how young she was when they first married. How through their marriage there had been many ups and downs, many good times and many difficult times. He remembered how his wife always said in the good times to thank God for them and how, in the difficult times, she said to ask God to give them the strength to thank Him for those too. He smiled as he thought of the expressions on her face when she would say this; expressions he loved.

"Are you awake, dear?" he heard his wife ask.

"Yes, I am, I hope I didn't wake you," he replied with concern. "No, you didn't," she said, as she turned to embrace him. "I couldn't sleep and I was just lying here thinking about our life together."

"So was I," responded the husband.

"I was thinking how God has been good to us and how you never forgot that, dear," explained the wife, gently.

"I was thinking the same about you!" exclaimed the

surprised husband. "Isn't it strange how we thought the same thing?"

"Not at all, dear," replied the wife, as she squeezed her husband. "Hearts that love God are often in tune with each other."

"Yes, we often have been, haven't we?" said the husband, thinking about the past.

"And we will continue to be," confirmed the wife.

Then as they lay there embracing each other both slipped into sleep with thoughts of their life together on their minds. As they slept the door to the bedroom opened quietly and a man looked in on the sleeping couple, then he closed the door, returning to his own bedroom where his wife was sitting up in the bed.

"Are they alright?" she asked.

"Yes, dear," replied the man, "they are both asleep with smiles on their faces."

"I hope we can be as happy as my grandparents when we have been married as long as they have," said the woman. "Yes, 60 years of marriage and they are so in love," stated the man. "Come to bed dear and let's say a little prayer together that our marriage can be like theirs," suggested the wife.

"I think it is all the prayers they have said through the years that have helped them stay in love."

"Well, if that's so we better make sure we pray every day because I want to stay in love with you," said the husband with a smile. "And I with you," responded the woman.

Then the two of them joined in prayer asking God to help them love each other eternally; a prayer that was heard and would be answered; a prayer that would be answered for all those who said it and meant it.

God the Father
>Marriage … A gift of love,
>to be lived in love so that it will grow in love.

Men and Women

St. Scholastica
>Men and women are called to holy lives. Lives created different by God and in those differences can the true beauty of God's love be found. It is in accepting these differences and by bowing to God's will in a person's life holiness can be attained.

Mistakes

Jesus
>Everyone makes mistakes, it is part of being a human. It is whether or not you learn from your mistakes that can make the difference between being wise or foolish.

St. Vincent Ferrer
>People make mistakes in life but if they cling to Jesus, Our Lord, seeking help to overcome their wrongs, even though people will continue to make mistakes, heaven will be their final resting place.

Money

Father
>The amount of money paid to some of those who entertain today is sinful when others starve, suffer and die because of the lack of food or medicine. The excess the few receive often comes at the expense of the many in need.

Mother Mary

St. Peter Chanel

Mother Mary walks with each person desiring only to bring them closer to God. Mother Mary opens her immaculate heart to each one so that united in her love each one can find the divine love that awaits them in the Most Sacred Heart of Jesus. Mother Mary gently leads all those who will allow her to do so to sanctification in the glory of God in heaven. Our heavenly Mother, our loving Mother, our holy Mother, Mary.

Father

By My Son, Jesus, becoming man through Mary, God became man and in doing so lifted mankind above the angels. God as man brought all of mankind into a sacred union, that when lived in the love it was given, truly makes every one who does so sacred.

Jesus

In the life of My Mother, Mary is an example
of how to love God with humility.

St. Theodosius

The Mother of God, so dear to Me.
The Mother of God, so loving to Me.
The Mother of God, so welcoming to Me.
Our Blessed Mother, Mary who wants to have
the same relationship with all of humanity.
John 19:27 your mother.

Mystery

Jesus

A mystery of My love is that the more of you love Me the more you want to and that want grows, never to be satisfied on earth.

God the Father

The mystery of the Trinity cannot be known on earth so just believe, accept and live in this truth.
Daniel 2:27 the mystery.

Needs

Jesus

The lives of all people are full of the same needs: to be loved, to love, to be secure and to have all they need to be happy. The answer for all people is the same and that is their needs can be fulfilled in Me. Any other answer is lacking completeness and any other answer truly is not fulfilling.
Lamentations 2:17 he has fulfilled.

Others

God the Father

In the face of another you can see the wonder of My creative love. In the face of another you can see the image of My gracious love. In the face of another you can see the love I have for mankind.
If only you look with a heart open to My love.

God the Father
>Try to see each person as a gift of My love to you
>and treasure them as you treasure My love.
>*Acts 8:20 the gift of God.*

God the Father
>The love you have for Me should bring you to love others.

God the Father
>It is easy to criticize others without thinking about the wrongs you have done. It is far better to show kindness and understanding, remembering how weak you are.

Jesus
>While others may offend you,
>you should try not to offend others.

God the Father
>Do not think the worst of others,
>always think and hope for the best.

Jesus
>To look upon another and to see how you can use them for your own satisfaction is wrong. To look upon another and to see how in Me you can love them is how you should look at all people at all times.

Jesus
>It does not matter what the race,
>what the colour or what the language,
>I love all people and so should you.

Jesus
>Be aware of the needs of others
>and try to help them be satisfied in Me.

Jesus
>While others embrace the world and sin,
>those who embrace Me have to carry more crosses.
>*Ezekiel 45:22 on behalf of all the people.*

St. Leo the Great
>The greater your love of God
>the greater your effect on the lives of others will be.

God the Father
>Do not condemn others for what you would do yourself
>otherwise in truth you are condemning yourself.

Jesus
>Trying not to hurt another because you love them is
>what you should be trying to do at all times to all people.

Pentecost

God the Father
>Today, the day My Holy Spirit breathed the fire of love into souls. Today, the day My Holy Spirit strengthened drooping hearts. Today, the day My Holy Spirit gifted the lives of those called to do My Will.
>If you seek the Holy Spirit every day then every day can be a Pentecost for you.

Pleasing to God

Jesus
> To please Me one only needs to be obedient to the commandments. All of them, not only the ones given through Moses, but also the ones I gave Myself to mankind.
> *John 6:36 I told you.*

God the Father
> To please Me, serve Me in love.
> To please Me, bring others to know My love.
> To please Me, be obedient to My will
> and most of all love Me, for this is most pleasing to Me.

Poverty

God the Father
> To help the poor is a necessity in the life of all Christians or how can they truly call themselves Christian?

Jesus
> There are many greedy people in the world
> and sadly because of this there are many poor.

God the Father
> Poverty of soul is the worst kind of poverty.

St. Clare
> It is a poor person indeed who does not want to share with their brothers and sisters.

Pride

St. Peter
>Mankind's pride is all that stops mankind from accepting God's will into their lives.
>*Luke 24:25 oh how foolish you are.*

God the Father
>The mighty will be brought low
>unless they are mighty in My love.

Priests

Jesus
>All priests are gifted. The difference between them at times is that some do not believe in the gifts or accept them, while others do.

Prisoners

St. Bartholomew
>People today are often trapped in their own little worlds which revolve around self. Lives like this are ones that are imprisoned. It's when people's lives revolve around God, loving Him, serving Him and loving others that freedom is found.

Remembering

St. John of God
>The Angelus is an important way of remembering Our Lord's coming to earth, a way that should not be forgotten.

Sacrifice

St. Agnes
> To follow Jesus means to be prepared to sacrifice
> at all times, not just when you feel that you should.

St. Peter Chanel
> Sometimes sacrifices are needed to open hearts to God
> and each sacrifice should be seen for what it is, a grace
> that God gives to people in His love.

Saints

God the Father
> There are future saints everywhere on earth,
> it is just they have not reached that state yet.
> *Ephesians 6:9 all the holy ones.*

Jesus
> One thing that unites all the saints lives on earth
> was their trust in Me. Be the same and follow in their
> footsteps: footsteps of faith.
> *Matthew 6:5 they have received their reward.*

Jesus
> When you think of the saints think of how I expressed
> My love through them and how the saints embraced My
> love in their lives.

God the Father
>In each saint My love has shone brightly bringing My glory into their lives. Today there are many in the world shining brightly in My love and again My glory is seen in these lives of future saints.
>*2 Corinthians 1:1 all the holy ones.*

God the Father
>The saints became saints through their perseverance and trust in Me. Anyone who does the same in their life will also become a saint.

St. Theresa Little Flower
>The saints in heaven pray for all people to know God's love so that all people can become beautiful roses in God's garden in heaven.

St. Cyril
>To be a saint look to heaven and do not let your gaze wander.

Jesus
>Saintly voices fill eternity with their prayers of love and adoration.

Jesus
>Listening to the saints is wise,
>it is something all mankind should do.

SALVATION

St. John of God
>One man, one God, one salvation … Jesus.

Jesus
> It is by the efforts of a few
> that many will find salvation in Me.

SERVICE

Jesus
> To serve Me in the way I want,
> a person must love in all situations.
> *Isaiah 65:13 my servants.*

God the Father
> Those who serve Me in love serve as they should.
> Those who serve Me begrudgingly as a duty serve themselves more crosses which they might not have the strength to carry and in the end may break under the strain and end up serving only evil.
> *Luke 3:5 the rough ways.*

God the Father
> To follow My Son, love.
> To serve My Son, love.
> To imitate My Son, love.
> Love Me, love your fellow man and love all that I have created. In doing so a person follows the life My Son, Jesus, lived on earth and imitates His servitude to My loving will.

God the Father
> Those who serve in government should remember they are there to serve God first, fellow man next and themselves last of all.

Jesus
> The way of serving Me may be hard
> but the way of serving sin is soul destroying.

Jesus
> If you walk in love, in truth, and in service of Me,
> you walk the way that will lead you to heaven.

Jesus
> A loving servant is loved and rewarded by His Lord.
> *Malachi 3:22 my servant.*

St. Leo the Great
> To be great in this world is meaningless in heaven
> unless it is greatness in serving God.

St. Thomas More
> To be a servant of Jesus you must serve in love
> and with humility.

SIN

God the Father
> Under no circumstance is sin or the approval of it
> acceptable to Me.

Jesus
> Be aware of sin and evil in the world and then
> understand in My love these cannot harm you.
> It is only in your weakness that they can.

God the Father
> You must at all times make allowances for others
> but at no time make allowances for their sins.

St. Stanislaus
> No matter who it is that sins, sin must never be accepted.
> *Isaiah 5:20 woe to those who call evil good and good evil.*

Jesus
> Never see sin as amusing for it never is.

God the Father
> The world is sinking in sin
> when it should be sailing in love.

Jesus
> Show tolerance to all that is not sinful, but show no tolerance to sin for in doing so you allow sin to grow.

Jesus
> Never give approval to sin,
> for in doing so you would sin yourself.
> *Sirach 47:24–25 their sinfulness grew more and more and they lent themselves to every evil.*

Sorrow

St. Brendan
> I shed tears of sorrow to see my nation tearing itself apart in sin. How easily the Irish today turn away from the faith their ancestors gave their very lives for. How sad the sacrifices of yesterday are forgotten and the reason for them seen as worthless.

Suffering

Jesus
>Every time you hurt and you offer it to me
>you are lifted closer to My cross.

The Church

St. Benedict
>The might of God is found in the Sacraments.
>The power of God is found in His love.
>The mighty church of God is filled with His power by the love of the Sacraments. Taking the Sacraments away leaves the other denominations empty and powerless.

Jesus
>No matter what the rite unless it is obedience to My Pope it must be in error to some degree.
>*Romans 13:1 for there is no authority except from God, and those that exist have been established by God.*
>*Romans 13:2 therefore, whoever resists authority opposes what God has appointed.*

St. Scholastica
>At the centre of all religious life must be obedience to God's will and obedience to His church. Without this a religious life means little at all and is religious in name only.
>*1 Corinthians 4:6 you will be inflated with pride.*

St. Scholastica
>To give oneself to God in love,
>To give oneself to God in service,
>To give oneself to God in obedience,
>Is the call to all the Church,
>any other call is the call of the world.
>*John 4:42 of the world.*

Jesus
>Just as Peter sat in the chair of My authority and love, so do all those who follow him as pope. This is a truth of heaven and it is a truth of earth that should be accepted by all.
>*Ephesians 1:10 in heaven and on earth.*

St. Peter
>When Our Lord, Jesus, gave me authority He gave me the authority to serve and not be served, to follow and not be followed, to be obedient to God's will and not to my own will.
>When Our Lord, Jesus, gives His grace to people on earth by welcoming them as part of His church, He expects them to bow to the authority of His church and to be obedient to His will by following the guidance of the one He has chosen to sit in my chair in Rome.
>*2 Peter 1:19 you will do well to be attentive to it.*
>*1 Peter 4:2 the will of God.*

Jesus

A united church is a strong church.
A divided church is a weak church.
Today the church is weakened by many divisions of pride.
Now is the time for the church to unite in humility
under obedience to My will and to My chosen successor
to Peter: the Pope.
1 Corin 14:33 all the churches.

God the Father

There is only one truth of God and so there should be
only one church of God. The truth is My Son, Jesus
and His church is the One Holy, Catholic and Apostolic
Church given through Peter and continuing through
Peter's successors.
1 Peter 1:22 obedience to the truth.
2 Corin 1:1 the church of God.

Jesus

My will on earth is found in the Holy Roman Catholic
Church and all those churches in obedience to My Pope.
1 Thessalonians 2:14 the churches of God.

Jesus

It does not matter what the rite is as long as the belief
in My true presence and obedience to My Pope is there,
then it truly is in communion with Me.

Jesus

To walk in My Spirit be obedient to My church
and to My Pope.

THE CROSS

St. Paul of the Cross
> In each wound of Christ, Our Lord, I saw the great love God has for mankind and in each one I saw how mankind in its pride inflicted these wounds upon its Lord.
> *1 Corinthians 1:18 the message of the cross.*

St. Paul of the Cross
> The crosses in life can be heavy
> when you carry them in self or lightened
> when you carry them in Christ, Our Lord.

Jesus
> The worthiness of a person to love Me is found
> in My love on the cross.
> *Romans 15:17 in Christ Jesus.*

Jesus
> How much more can I reveal My love for mankind than dying on the cross for their sins?

Jesus
> As I open My arms to embrace My cross and offer My life to the Father so must My followers embrace their crosses and offer their lives in love to the Father if they truly want to imitate Me.

THE END OF TIME

Jesus
> The end of time will come when My Father commands it, not when people want it to be.

St. Paul
>It is wiser to live each moment as if it is your last one on earth rather than to worry about when the world will end and in your fear do little at all.

The Eucharist

Jesus
>Whatever language the Eucharist is celebrated in is not so important. It is the holiness, the reverence and the opening of oneself to Me in the Holy Mass that are important.

The Faith

God the Father
>The guaranteed way to find eternal peace in heaven is to live the holy Catholic faith without changing or denying any aspect of it.
>
>*2 Corinthians 1:24 stand firm in the faith.*

St. Patrick
>Ireland can be a bastion of the faith once more, it only needs the people to see the wrongs they now embrace and then to reject them.

Jesus
>If a person denies the commandments My Father gave, denies My sacrifice and My resurrection, denies the truth of the teachings of the church, then even though the person may be baptized, by these denials the person no longer can claim to be a Christian, for in truth they are not.

God the Father
>It is by living the Catholic faith given to mankind by My Son, Jesus, through Peter, His chosen leader, and passed on through Peter's successors, that a person can be sure of reaching eternal love in heaven.
>*Matthew 5:12 your reward will be great in heaven.*

Jesus
>Whatever the faith, unless a person knows Me, it is an empty faith.

The Future

Jesus
>Many evil people have come to power throughout history and brought pain and suffering with them. The future will be no different unless people stand firm in My love and do not accept the ways that bring evil to positions of power.
>*Isaiah 46:8 remember this and be firm.*

Jesus
>It is a certain future for those who love Me and obey My commands.
>It is an uncertain future for those who do not.
>*Matthew 28:20 observe all that I have commanded.*

The Hands of Christ

St. Benedict
>If you place yourself into the hands of Christ, Our Lord, there is nothing evil can do to harm your soul, for it is protected by the all powerful.

The Love of God

God the Father
> In every moment is the love I have placed there and in every moment is the choice to live in that love or not.
> *Ezekiel 37:24 live by my statutes and carefully observe my decrees.*

Jesus
> The love of God is more obvious in those who are gentle, generous and kind.

St. Teresa of Avila
> Love will overcome even the fiercest opposition for nothing can stand in the way of love; the love of God.

God the Father
> In the beginning was love.
> In the end will be love.
> In between there is love.
> This is the truth that sadly many are blind to and in their blindness turn away from love and into the grasp of evil.
> *John 1:1 in the beginning.*
> *Revelations 1:8 the one who is and who was and who is to come, the almighty.*
> *Titus 3:4 love of God.*

St. Philip Neri
> To attract people to the love of God
> you must try to live as an image of His love;
> an image of Jesus.

God the Father
> In all the world is My love but sadly many do not see or believe this and so live outside of My love and in an empty world.

Jesus
> The price you pay for loving Me is to spend eternity in My love and to be filled with the joy of My love in every eternal moment.

THE PERSON

Jesus
> Your mind, your body and your soul are one, not separate. All need to develop in My grace and cannot achieve their full potential when this is forgotten.

St. Francis of Assisi
> God can create a new life for all people if only they want it and are prepared to accept the changes needed in their present life.

St. Catherine of Sienna
> When you give your person to Christ
> His personality is seen in your life.
> *Philip 3:12 since I have indeed been taken possession of by Christ.*

THE POWER OF GOD

St. Benedict
>The power that God bestows upon a person who loves Him and is prepared to give their all to serve and glorify God is beyond the understanding of mankind but should be believed in by mankind.
>*Luke 1:35 the power of the most high.*

St. Mark
>The word of God is all powerful;
>live to His word and be filled with that power.
>*1 Corinthians 2:5 so that your faith may not rest on human wisdom but on the power of God.*

Holy Spirit
>With My power in their heart
>a person can do anything that is good.

Jesus
>Just as the might of Rome succumbed to My love so will all empires that man creates succumb and fall to the power of My love.

THE ROSARY

God the Father
>The power of the rosary is the power of My Son's love through the heart of His immaculate, holy and humble Mother, Mary.
>*Luke 2:34 Mary His mother.*

THE SICK

Jesus
Some people are incapable of looking after themselves. Others in these cases must take the responsibility of doing so. If not, then society has turned its back on those in need and turned its back on the commandment to love one another.
1 Corin 16:1 so give recognition to such people.
Sirach 39:16 every need is supplied.

God the Father
The sick at times cannot do what the healthy can.
In these moments understand their weakness and help them. Do not condemn or reject them.

THE TRUTH

Jesus
There is but one truth, I am that truth and anything that denies, rejects or excludes My truth is in the wrong.

Jesus
The truth at times may seem a difficult path to walk but remember it is the only path that leads to Me.

Jesus
The truth is hard to live at times
but the alternative is even harder eternally.

God the Father
> What is true must never be denied
> or you risk living in deceit.
> *Sirach 7:6 and mar your integrity.*

God the Father
> The honest way is the only way to succeed in Me.
> *Isaiah 44:25 I bring to nought the omens of liars.*

Jesus
> The complete truth on earth is the Catholic truth,
> for it is My truth.

The Victory

St. Benedict
> Evil is defeated never doubt that, for if you do then you doubt in the victorious sacrifice of Jesus, Our Lord.

God the Father
> My Son, Jesus has defeated evil on the cross. It is mankind's refusal to accept this victory that keeps evil alive in the world today.

God the Father
> It may seem at times as if evil and wrong doers are triumphing but trust Me this is not so. Evil has been defeated on the cross by My Son, Jesus, and wrong will never triumph for the eternal victory is with My Son, Jesus, and His followers. Anyone who denies this, rejects this and turns away from this may find that they have only triumphed in bringing upon themselves eternal suffering and damnation.

St. Michael the Archangel
>To carry the banner of God's victory in your life openly and without fear will bring His victory into the hearts of others.
>*Revelations 3:5 the victor.*

God the Father
>Remember, fight evil with love, compassion and understanding, for it is in this way you will find victory; the way of Jesus, My Son.

The Way

Jesus
>The way to true happiness is found in Me.
>The way to eternal peace is found in Me.
>The way to a life of eternal happiness and a never-ending peace is found in Me.
>I am the way and there is no other.
>*John 14:6 I am the way.*
>*Proverbs 26:5 according to his folly.*

Through the Apostles

St. Mark
>Through the apostles I came to know God in a deeper way. It is the same for all people, if they too look to the apostles each person can come to a deeper relationship with Jesus, Our Lord, by the grace He bestowed upon and through the apostles.

St. Andrew
>The apostolic life should be the life of every Christian.

TRUTH

Jesus
>When others are blind to the truth
>it is with love you will open their eyes and their hearts.
>*Acts 12:10 opened for them.*

St. Sebastian
>To stand for the truth of God may bring suffering in this life on earth but it brings great glory in the life to come in heaven.
>*Isaiah 62:3 a glorious crown.*

Jesus
>The just shall be rewarded.
>The honest shall be received in grace.
>The truthful shall be glorified.
>In My grace all those who profess the truth honestly shall be justified and receive eternal glory as their reward.

Jesus
>Words of truth are needed today but they are needed with love not judgment or condemnation.
>*Psalm 15:2 speaking truth from the heart.*

God the Father
>With My truth comes a life of freedom for those who accept to live in it.

God the Father
>The truth can never be changed no matter what the reason for then it is no longer the truth.

Jesus
> Those who see the truth must help the blind
> to find true sight also.
> *Psalm 79:10 our eyes make clear.*

TRUST

God the Father
> The way of mankind is often to mistrust rather than to trust. When it is this way suspicions lead to fears and fears can lead to offences against one another. Mankind needs to start trusting again and also living up to that trust if it is to find security and peace. Trust in God and trust in one another.

God the Father
> It is in the trying moments
> you must try to trust in Me completely.

UNITED

God the Father
> When a person prays in love to Me their prayers unite with all others who throughout time have prayed in love to Me. Yet at the same time their prayers remain separate, individual and part of a personal relationship with Me.

God the Father
> A soul in love with Me unites with all the other souls in love with Me throughout time to make a sweet chorus of love that brings joy to My heart.

Violence

Jesus
> Violence should never entertain for when it does the one being entertained is being drawn into sin when they enjoy the evil that is in violence and enjoy its content.

Weakness

God the Father
> Do not lose heart over what others do. See in their mistakes that people need help in overcoming their weaknesses and by showing love at all times help them to.

Wisdom

God the Father
> It is love of God that separates the wise from the foolish.

St. Elizabeth
> With true wisdom comes love,
> for how can one be wise without love.

St. Benedict
> It is the wise who love God and the foolish who do not.

Worry

God the Father
> With worry on your heart it is easy to let fear in. Remember the only thing worry can change is you ... for it can weaken your trust in Me.

Jesus
>Worry only increases problems,
>it is trust in Me that will decrease them.

WORSHIP

St. Michael the Archangel
>As I kneel before God I pray that all of mankind would join me in worship of the Divine Lord.

Books available from:

U.S.A.

Alan Ames Ministry
PO Box 200
340 Belvedere Ave
Kellogg
Minnesota 55945
Phone: 507 767 3027
Web: http://www.alanames.org

Australia

Touch of Heaven
(Alan Ames Ministry)
PO Box 85
Wembley, 6014
West Australia
Phone: 61 89275 6608
Fax: 61 89382 4392
Web: http://www.alanames.ws
Email: touchofheaven@iinet.net.au